Jams, Jellies, Pickles & More

201 EASY IDEAS FOR CANNING & PRESERVING

TASTE OF HOME BOOKS • RDA ENTHUSIAST BRANDS, LLC • MILWAUKEE, WI

A TASTE OF HOME/READER'S DIGEST BOOK

EDITORIAL

Editor-in-Chief: Catherine Cassidy
Creative Director: Howard Greenberg
Editorial Operations Director: Kerri Balliet

Managing Editor, Print & Digital Books:
Mark Hagen
Associate Creative Director: Edwin Robles Jr.

Editor: Janet Briggs
Art Director: Jessie Sharon
Layout Designer: Catherine Fletcher
Editorial Production Manager: Dena Ahlers
Copy Chief: Deb Warlaumont Mulvey
Copy Editor: Kaitlin Stainbrook
Content Operations Manager: Colleen King
Content Operations Assistant: Shannon Stroud
Executive Assistant: Marie Brannon

Chief Food Editor: Karen Berner
Food Editors: James Schend; Peggy Woodward, RD
Recipe Editors: Mary King; Jenni Sharp, RD; Irene Yeh

Test Kitchen & Food Styling Manager:
Sarah Thompson
Test Cooks: Nicholas Iverson (lead),
Matthew Hass, Lauren Knoelke
Food Stylists: Kathryn Conrad (senior),
Leah Rekau, Shannon Roum
Prep Cooks: Megumi Garcia, Melissa Hansen,
Bethany Van Jacobson, Sara Wirtz

Photography Director: Stephanie Marchese
Photographers: Dan Roberts, Jim Wieland
Photographer/Set Stylist: Grace Natoli Sheldon
Set Stylists: Stacey Genaw, Melissa Haberman,
Dee Dee Jacq
Photo Studio Assistant: Ester Robards

Editorial Business Manager: Kristy Martin
Editorial Business Associate: Samantha Lea Stoeger

BUSINESS

Vice President, Chief Sales Officer:
Mark S. Josephson

General Manager, Taste of Home Cooking School:
Erin Puariea

THE READER'S DIGEST ASSOCIATION, INC.

President and Chief Executive Officer:
Bonnie Kintzer
Chief Financial Officer: Colette Chestnut
**Vice President, Chief Operating Officer,
North America:** Howard Halligan
Vice President, Enthusiast Brands, Books & Retail:
Harold Clarke
Vice President, North American Operations:
Philippe Cloutier
Chief Marketing Officer: Leslie Dukker Doty
Vice President, North American Human Resources:
Phyllis E. Gebhardt, SPHR
Vice President, Brand Marketing: Beth Gorry
Vice President, Global Communications: Susan Russ
Vice President, North American Technology:
Aneel Tejwaney
Vice President, Consumer Marketing Planning:
Jim Woods

For other Taste of Home books and products,
visit us at tasteofhome.com.

For more Reader's Digest products and information,
visit rd.com (in the United States) or rd.ca (in Canada).

International Standard Book Number:
978-1-61765-366-7
Library of Congress Control Number:
2014948115

Cover Photographer: Dan Roberts
Set Stylist: Melissa Haberman
Food Stylist: Shannon Roum

Pictured on front cover:
Orange Jelly, page 104
Pictured on back cover:
Cider Jelly, page 18 and
Grandma's Dill Pickles, page 60
Illustrations on inside cover:
Ohn Mar/Shutterstock.com

Printed in China.
1 3 5 7 9 10 8 6 4 2

LIKE US
facebook.com/tasteofhome

TWEET US
@tasteofhome

FOLLOW US
pinterest.com/taste_of_home

SHOP WITH US
shoptasteofhome.com

SHARE A RECIPE
tasteofhome.com/submit

Plum Anise Jam,
page 18

Christmas Pickles, page 121

TABLE OF CONTENTS

Zesty
Lemon Curd,
page 173

Mild Tomato
Salsa,
page 67

Savor the Taste of Summer Year Round

Summer is the best time to indulge in juicy fruits and crisp veggies. Whether you purchase them from earthy stands at farmers markets, pull them from colorful displays at grocery stores or pick them fresh from your garden, it's easy to end up with more produce than you need.

That's not a problem with *Taste of Home Jams, Jellies, Pickles & More!* After all, this delightful collection helps you preserve summer flavor for year-round enjoyment. If you've never canned or preserved before, the step-by-step directions found here make it a breeze. If you're an experienced canner, you'll delight in these finger-licking recipes, handy tips and gorgeous photos. So what are you waiting for? Let's get canning and preserving today!

Try this
Lime Mint Jelly
on page 26.

Tips for Successful Canning:

This book focuses on hot water bath canning, which is used to process high-acid foods such as tomatoes, fruits, pickles, jams and other preserves. Remember these tips when canning:

SELECT FRUITS and vegetables when they are at the peak of their quality and flavor, and wash them thoroughly before using.

FOLLOW DIRECTIONS for each recipe exactly—don't substitute ingredients or change processing times. Prepare only one recipe at a time; do not double recipes.

SUBSTITUTE A CAKE COOLING RACK if you don't have a rack specifically made for canning. Place rack in the canner before you add the canning jars.

USE A CANNING FUNNEL that has a wide opening and sits on the inside of the mouth of the jar, allowing you to fill jars cleanly and easily. Wipe the threads and rim of each jar to remove any food that spills.

REUSE SCREW BANDS if they are not warped or rusty. Jar lids are not reusable, however, so use a new one for each of your canned creations.

ACCURATELY MEASURE the headspace—the distance between the top of the jar and the food/liquid. This is critical because it affects how well the jar seals and preserves its contents. A clear plastic ruler—kept solely for kitchen use—is a big help in determining the correct headspace.

REFRIGERATE ANY LEFTOVERS that won't completely fill another jar. Use the leftovers within the next few days.

USE NONMETALLIC UTENSILS when removing air bubbles from the jar and measuring headspace.

STORE HOME-CANNED FOODS in your cupboard for up to one year.

Tools of the Trade

Here's what you need to get started using the hot water bath processing method.

1. LARGE STOCKPOT: Choose a stockpot that holds at least 12 quarts and is tall enough to allow the jars to be fully submerged.

2. LADLE: Be careful when pouring hot mixtures into jars or jar funnels.

3. JAR FUNNEL: Place in the mouth of the jar to fill without spilling.

4. MAGNETIC LID LIFTER: Lift lids out of hot water using this tool's magnetic end.

**5. BUBBLE REMOVER &
HEADSPACE TOOL:** Slide this tool down the side of filled jars to release air bubbles and measure headspace.

6. JAR WRENCH: Jar lids can be difficult to turn without this wrench.

7. TONGS (WITH COATED HANDLES): You'll need tongs to lift foods during cooking and canning.

8. JAR LIFTER: Safely remove hot jars from boiling water with one hand.

9. GLASS CANNING JARS, LIDS & BANDS: Fill the glass jars, then seal with one-time-use lids and reusable bands.

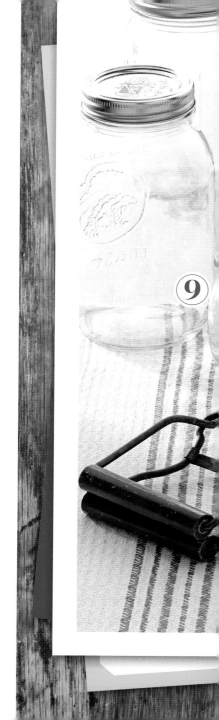

SEAL
the Deal

Enjoy this year's harvest well into next year.

You have your tools...you've read the tips... and you're all set to put up summer's bounty. Or, are you?

Before you dive in, take a quick moment to review the basic steps for canning and processing. Next, select the recipe that's right for you, your produce and your taste. Then—let's get canning!

BEFORE YOU START

Before you begin canning, read the recipe instructions and gather all equipment and ingredients. Inspect the glass canning jars carefully for any chips, cracks, uneven rims or sharp edges that may prevent sealing or cause breakage. Discard any imperfect jars.

Wash the jars, bands and lids in hot soapy water; rinse thoroughly. (You also can use a dishwasher.)

HOT & STERILIZED JARS

For hot jars, place the jars in a large kettle. Fill the jars and kettle with hot (not boiling) water that covers the jars by 1 inch; bring to a simmer over medium-low heat.

For sterilized jars, start by following the directions above, but bring the water to a boil. After boiling the jars for 10 minutes, turn the heat down so the water is at a simmer.

STERILIZED VS. HOT JARS
There's a reason *some canning recipes call for hot sterilized jars while others call simply for hot jars.* If the mixture will be processed for 10-plus minutes up to 1,000 feet above sea level, jars just need to be hot. If the processing time is shorter, jars must be sterilized in boiling water for 10 minutes. (Add 1 minute for each 1,000 feet of additional altitude.)

For lids (hot jars and sterilized jars), heat water on low in a small saucepan. Add lids. Keep jars and lids in the hot water until ready to use. Bands just need to be dry and ready to use.

When you're ready to fill the jars, remove them with a jar lifter, emptying water into the kettle. Set the jars and lids on a clean kitchen towel.

WHAT YOU NEED

- ☐ Large Stockpot
- ☐ Ladle
- ☐ Jar Funnel
- ☐ Magnetic Lid Lifter
- ☐ Bubble Remover & Headspace Tool
- ☐ Jar Wrench
- ☐ Tongs
- ☐ Jar Lifter
- ☐ Canning Jars, Lids & Bands

Fill Jars & Process

1. Prepare the recipe as directed. Ladle or pour the hot mixture into the prepared jars. Use a ruler to make sure you're leaving the recommended amount of headspace for expansion during processing.

2. Remove air bubbles by sliding a nonmetallic utensil between the food and inside of the jar two or three times. Wipe the threads and rim of the jar with a clean, damp cloth. Place a warm lid on top of each jar with the sealing compound next to the glass.

3. Screw a band onto the jar just until you feel resistance.

4. Immediately after filling each jar, use a jar lifter to place the jar onto the canning rack, making sure the jars are not touching. Using the handles on the rack, lower the filled rack into the canner. Add enough boiling water to

the canner to cover jars by 1 to 2 inches. Cover the canner; adjust the heat to hold a steady rolling boil. Start counting the processing time when the water returns to a boil. If water level decreases while processing, add more boiling water.

5. When the processing time is complete, turn off the heat and remove canner lid. Let canner cool for 5 minutes before removing jars. Using jar lifter, remove jars and set them upright, 1 to 2 inches apart, on a dry towel to cool for 12-24 hours.

6. After jars have cooled, test each lid to determine if it sealed by pressing the center of the lid. If the lid is not sealed, do not reprocess. Store the jar in the refrigerator and eat the contents within several days.

7. Wipe jars clean, label and date. Store in a cool, dry, dark place for up to one year.

Jams & Jellies

❋ The processing times listed for all the recipes in this chapter are for altitudes of 1,000 feet or less. Add 1 minute to the proceesing time for each 1,000 feet of additional altitude.

BLUEBERRY JELLY

My mother brought this old family recipe with her when she moved here from Scotland. My children and husband especially love spreading this delectable jelly on slices of homemade bread.

—ELAINE SOPER TRINITY BAY, NL

PREP: 1¼ HOURS • **PROCESS:** 5 MIN.
MAKES: 6 PINTS

- 2 **quarts fresh or frozen blueberries**
- 4 **cups water**
- 12 **cups sugar**
- 2 **pouches (3 ounces each) liquid fruit pectin**

1. Place blueberries in a Dutch oven and crush slightly. Add water; bring to a boil. Reduce heat to medium; cook, uncovered, for 45 minutes. Line a strainer with four layers of cheesecloth and place over a bowl. Place berry mixture in strainer; cover with edges of cheesecloth. Let stand for 30 minutes or until liquid measures 6 cups.

2. Pour juice back into Dutch oven; gradually stir in sugar until it dissolves. Bring to a boil over high heat, stirring constantly. Stir in pectin. Continue to boil 1 minute, stirring constantly.

3. Remove from heat; skim off foam. Ladle hot mixture into six hot sterilized 1-pint jars, leaving ¼-in. headspace. Wipe rims. Center lids on jars; screw on bands until fingertip tight.

4. Place jars into canner with simmering water, ensuring that they are completely covered with water. Bring to a boil; process for 5 minutes. Remove jars and cool.

CINNAMON PLUM JAM

When I share this slightly sweet jam with family and friends, it disappears quickly.

—**ELOISE NEELEY** NORTON, OH

PREP: 15 MIN. • **PROCESS:** 10 MIN.
MAKES: 7 HALF-PINTS

- 7 **cups sugar**
- 5 **cups coarsely ground peeled plums (about 2½ pounds)**
- ½ **cup water**
- ⅓ **cup bottled lemon juice**
- 1 **package (1¾ ounces) powdered fruit pectin**
- ½ **teaspoon ground cinnamon**

1. In a Dutch oven, combine sugars, plums, water and lemon juice. Bring to a full rolling boil, stirring constantly. Stir in pectin. Continue to boil 1 minute, stirring constantly.

2. Remove from heat; stir in cinnamon. Skim off foam. Ladle hot mixture into seven hot half-pint jars, leaving ¼-in. headspace. Remove air bubbles and adjust headspace, if necessary, by adding hot mixture. Wipe rims. Center lids on jars; screw on bands until fingertip tight.

3. Place the jars into canner with simmering water, ensuring that they are completely covered with water. Bring to a boil; process for 10 minutes. Remove jars and cool.

BLACKBERRY APPLE JELLY

PREP: 45 MIN. • **PROCESS:** 5 MIN.
MAKES: 9 HALF-PINTS

- 3 **pounds blackberries (about 2½ quarts)**
- 1¼ **cups water**
- 7 **to 8 medium apples**
  Additional water
  Bottled apple juice, optional
- ¼ **cup bottled lemon juice**
- 8 **cups sugar**
- 2 **pouches (3 ounces each) liquid fruit pectin**

1. In a Dutch oven, bring blackberries and water to a boil. Reduce heat; simmer 5 minutes. Line a strainer with four layers of cheesecloth and place over a bowl. Place berry mixture in strainer; cover with edges of cheesecloth. Let stand 30 minutes or until strained, reserving juice and discarding pulp.

2. Remove and discard stems and blossom ends from apples (do not pare or core); cut into small pieces. Place in the Dutch oven; add just enough water to cover. Bring to a boil. Reduce heat; simmer 20 minutes or until apples are tender. Strain through a cheesecloth-lined strainer, reserving juice and discarding pulp.

3. Measure the reserved blackberry and apple juices; return to the pan. If necessary, add water or bottled apple juice to equal 4 cups. Stir in lemon juice, then sugar. Bring to a full rolling boil over high heat, stirring constantly. Stir in the pectin. Continue to boil 1 minute, stirring constantly.

4. Remove from heat; skim off foam. Carefully ladle hot mixture into nine hot sterilized half-pint jars, leaving ¼-in. headspace. Wipe rims. Center lids on jars; screw on bands until fingertip tight.

5. Place the jars into canner with simmering water, ensuring that they are completely covered with water. Bring to a boil; process for 5 minutes. Remove jars and cool.

The apples in this jam come from our old-fashioned orchard, while the blackberries grow wild along our creek. It's so popular, the jelly is usually gone by January! **—LIZ ENDACOTT** MATSQUI, BC

HONEY LEMON JELLY

I love both honey and lemon, so I combined those ingredients into a doubly delightful jelly. Spread it on toast, bagels, or English muffins for a tangy breakfast treat.

—RAMONA WYSONG BARLOW, KY

PREP: 50 MIN. • **PROCESS:** 5 MIN.
MAKES: 3 HALF-PINTS

- 2½ **cups honey**
- ¾ **cup lemon juice**
- 6 **tablespoons grated lemon peel**
- 1 **pouch (3 ounces) liquid fruit pectin**

1. In a Dutch oven, combine honey, lemon juice and peel. Bring to a full rolling boil over high heat, stirring constantly. Stir in pectin. Continue to boil 1 minute, stirring constantly.

2. Remove from heat; skim off foam. Ladle hot mixture into three hot sterilized half-pint jars, leaving ¼-in. headspace. Wipe the rims. Center lids on jars; screw on the bands until fingertip tight.

3. Place the jars into canner with simmering water, ensuring that they are completely covered with water. Bring to a boil; process for 5 minutes. Remove jars and cool.

RHUBARB-ORANGE MARMALADE

PREP: 2 HOURS + CHILLING
PROCESS: 10 MIN.
MAKES: 7 HALF-PINTS

- 6 **cups diced fresh or frozen rhubarb**
- 6 **cups sugar, divided**
- 2 **medium oranges**
- 1 **cup coarsely chopped walnuts**
- 1 **cup raisins**

1. In a large bowl, combine rhubarb and 4 cups sugar; cover and refrigerate overnight.

2. Peel rind from oranges; cut into very thin strips, about 1 in. long. Place strips in a small bowl; cover with boiling water. Let stand 30 minutes; drain. Trim white pith from oranges; discard pith. Cut oranges into ½-in. chunks, reserving juices. Discard membranes and seeds.

3. In a Dutch oven, combine rhubarb mixture, orange peel, orange chunks with juices, walnuts, raisins and remaining sugar. Bring to a boil. Reduce heat; simmer, uncovered, 1 to 1½ hours or until thickened.

4. Remove from heat; skim off foam. Carefully ladle hot mixture into seven hot half-pint jars, leaving ¼-in. headspace. Remove air bubbles and adjust headspace, if necessary, by adding hot mixture. Wipe rims. Center lids on jars; screw on the bands until fingertip tight.

5. Place the jars into canner with simmering water, ensuring that they are completely covered with water. Bring to a boil; process for 10 minutes. Remove jars and cool.

Rhubarb and orange make a great combination in this versatile marmalade. It's a perfect glaze for meat or poultry and tasty on toast.
—**JOAN MARKYTAN**
ELYSIAN, MN

CELESTIAL CHERRY CONSERVE

This recipe produces a rich, concentrated flavor that works perfectly on toast, ice cream or cheesecake. I also have had great results when substituting strawberries, blueberries, mango and complementary herbal teas.

—MAUREEN DELVES KAMLOOPS, BC

PREP: 40 MIN. • **PROCESS:** 5 MIN.
MAKES: 6 HALF-PINTS

- 2 **medium oranges**
- 6 **cups fresh dark sweet cherries, pitted**
- 3½ **cups sugar**
- 6 **tablespoons lemon juice**
- 4 **individual black cherry or wild berry herbal tea bags**
- 1 **cup boiling water**
- 1 **pouch (3 ounces) liquid fruit pectin**

1. Grate zest from the oranges; set zest aside. Peel oranges and discard peel; chop the oranges. In a large saucepan, combine cherries, sugar, lemon juice and chopped oranges. Bring to a boil. Reduce heat; simmer, uncovered, 6-8 minutes or until slightly thickened.
2. Meanwhile, place tea bags in a small bowl. Add boiling water. Cover and steep 5-6 minutes. Discard tea bags; add liquid to cherry mixture. Bring to a full rolling boil over high heat, stirring constantly. Stir in pectin. Boil 1 minute, stirring constantly.
3. Remove from heat; skim off foam. Ladle hot mixture into six hot sterilized half-pint jars, leaving ¼-in. headspace. Remove air bubbles and adjust headspace, if necessary, by adding hot mixture. Wipe rims. Center lids on jars; screw on bands until fingertip tight.
4. Place the jars into canner with simmering water, ensuring that they are completely covered with water. Bring to a boil; process for 5 minutes. Remove jars and cool.

FOOD TRIVIA!
Dark sweet cherries are good for you, so indulge! Lambert and Bing cherries are the commonly available dark or black sweet cherries. They are antioxidant rich, high in fiber and are a source of Vitamins A and C, iron and calcium.

CARROT CAKE JAM

For a change of pace from berry jams, try this unique option. Spread on a bagel with cream cheese; it tastes almost as good as real carrot cake!

—**RACHELLE STRATTON** ROCK SPRINGS, WY

PREP: 45 MIN. • **PROCESS:** 5 MIN.
MAKES: 8 HALF-PINTS

- 1 can (20 ounces) unsweetened crushed pineapple, undrained
- 1½ cups shredded carrots
- 1½ cups chopped peeled ripe pears
- 3 tablespoons lemon juice
- 1 teaspoon ground cinnamon
- ¼ teaspoon ground cloves
- ¼ teaspoon ground nutmeg
- 1 package (1¾ ounces) powdered fruit pectin
- 6½ cups sugar

1. In a large saucepan, combine the first seven ingredients. Bring to a boil. Reduce heat; cover and simmer for 15-20 minutes or until pears are tender, stirring occasionally. Stir in pectin. Bring to a full rolling boil over high heat, stirring constantly. Stir in sugar; return to a full rolling boil. Boil and stir 1 minute.

2. Remove from heat; skim off foam. Ladle hot mixture into eight hot sterilized half-pint jars, leaving ¼-in. headspace. Remove air bubbles and adjust headspace, if necessary, by adding hot mixture. Wipe the rims. Center lids on jars; screw on bands until fingertip tight.

3. Place the jars into canner with simmering water, ensuring that they are completely covered with water. Bring to a boil; process for 5 minutes. Remove jars and cool.

CRAN-RASPBERRY JAM

I'm sure to pick up extra bags of cranberries for the freezer in fall so that I can make this delicious jam all year round. My kids love it on peanut butter sandwiches. Jars of this ruby-colored jam also make great gifts.

—**MARJILEE BOOTH** CHINO HILLS, CA

PREP: 20 MIN. • **PROCESS:** 10 MIN.
MAKES: 6 HALF-PINTS

- 2 packages (10 ounces each) frozen sweetened raspberries, thawed
- 4 cups fresh or frozen cranberries
- 1 package (1¾ ounces) powdered fruit pectin
- 5 cups sugar

1. Drain raspberries, reserving juice; add enough water to juice to measure 1½ cups. Pour into a Dutch oven. Add raspberries and cranberries; stir in pectin. Bring to a full rolling boil over high heat, stirring constantly. Stir in sugar; return to a full rolling boil. Boil and stir for 1 minute.

2. Remove from heat; skim off foam. Ladle hot mixture into six hot half-pint jars, leaving ¼-in. headspace. Remove air bubbles and adjust headspace, if necessary, by adding the hot mixture. Wipe rims. Center lids on jars; screw on bands until fingertip tight.

3. Place the jars into canner with simmering water, ensuring that they are completely covered with water. Bring to a boil; process for 10 minutes. Remove jars and cool.

PLUM ANISE JAM

Growing up, my father loved black licorice and all my siblings and I loved it as well. I still enjoy the flavor of black licorice, but I can't eat the candy anymore because of health reasons. This recipe reminds me of the flavor I miss. The delicious jam tastes great with Brie or goat cheese and crackers.

—**JILL GRUENINGER** MEQUON, WI

PREP: 35 MIN.
PROCESS: 10 MIN.
MAKES: 8 HALF-PINTS

- 8 **cups chopped unpeeled fresh plums (about 3½ pounds)**
- ½ **cup water**
- 1 **package (1¾ ounces) pectin for lower sugar recipes**
- 1 **teaspoon butter**
- 4½ **cups sugar**
- 1 **tablespoon aniseed, crushed**

1. In a Dutch oven, combine the plums and water; bring to a boil. Reduce heat; simmer, covered, 5-7 minutes or until plums are softened.
2. Stir in pectin and butter. Bring to a full rolling boil over high heat, stirring constantly. Stir in sugar; return to a full rolling boil. Boil and stir 1 minute. Stir in aniseed.
3. Remove from heat; skim off foam. Ladle the hot mixture into eight hot half-pint jars, leaving ¼-in. headspace. Remove air bubbles and adjust the headspace, if necessary, by adding hot mixture. Wipe rims. Center lids on jars; screw on the bands until fingertip tight.
4. Place the jars into canner with simmering water, ensuring that they are completely covered with water. Bring to a boil; process for 10 minutes. Remove jars and cool.

CIDER JELLY

For a tasty jam during the fall, try this one using cider. The candy adds a delightful cinnamon flavor.

—**DONNA BENSEND** DALLAS, WI

PREP: 10 MIN.
PROCESS: 10 MIN.
MAKES: 6 HALF-PINTS

- 1 **quart unfiltered apple cider or juice**
- ⅔ **cup red hots candy**
- 1 **package (1¾ ounces) powdered fruit pectin**
- 5 **cups sugar**

1. In a Dutch oven, combine cider and red hots. Stir in pectin. Bring to a full rolling boil over high heat, stirring constantly. Stir in sugar; return to a full rolling boil. Boil and stir 1 minute.
2. Remove from heat; skim off foam. Ladle hot mixture into six hot half-pint jars, leaving ¼-in. headspace. Wipe the rims. Center lids on jars; screw on bands until fingertip tight.
3. Place the jars into canner with simmering water, ensuring that they are completely covered with water. Bring to a boil; process for 10 minutes. Remove jars and cool.

OVER-THE-TOP CHERRY JAM

We live in Door County, an area known for its wonderful tart cherries. This brilliant-colored sweet jam makes a lovely gift.

—KAREN HAEN STURGEON BAY, WI

PREP: 35 MIN. • **PROCESS:** 5 MIN.
MAKES: 6 HALF-PINTS

- 2½ **pounds fresh tart cherries, pitted**
- 1 **package (1¾ ounces) powdered fruit pectin**
- ½ **teaspoon butter**
- 4¾ **cups sugar**

1. In a food processor, cover and process cherries in batches until finely chopped. Transfer to a Dutch oven; stir in pectin and butter. Bring to a full rolling boil over high heat, stirring constantly. Stir in sugar; return to a full rolling boil. Boil and stir 1 minute.

2. Remove from heat; skim off foam. Ladle hot mixture into six hot sterilized half-pint jars, leaving ¼-in. headspace. Remove air bubbles and adjust the headspace, if necessary, by adding hot mixture. Wipe rims. Center lids on jars; screw on bands until fingertip tight.

3. Place the jars into canner with simmering water, ensuring that they are completely covered with water. Bring to a boil; process for 5 minutes. Remove jars and cool.

WATERMELON JELLY

With its beautiful shade of orange and intense watermelon flavor, this jelly lets you enjoy summer long after the cool weather arrives.

—TASTE OF HOME TEST KITCHEN

PREP: 25 MIN. + STANDING
PROCESS: 10 MIN.
MAKES: 5 HALF-PINTS

- **6 cups seeded chopped watermelon**
- **5 cups sugar**
- **⅓ cup white wine vinegar or white balsamic vinegar**
- **¼ cup lemon juice**
- **2 to 3 drops red food coloring, optional**
- **2 pouches (3 ounces each) liquid fruit pectin**

1. Place the watermelon in a food processor; cover and process until pureed. Line a strainer with four layers of cheesecloth and place over a bowl. Place pureed watermelon in prepared strainer; cover with the edges of cheesecloth. Let stand 10 minutes or until liquid measures 2 cups.

2. Discard watermelon pulp from cheesecloth; place liquid in a large saucepan. Stir in sugar, vinegar, lemon juice and if desired, food coloring. Bring to a full rolling boil over high heat, stirring constantly. Stir in pectin. Continue to boil 1 minute, stirring constantly.

3. Remove from heat; skim off foam. Ladle hot mixture into five hot half-pint jars, leaving ¼-in. headspace. Wipe the rims. Center lids on jars; screw on bands until fingertip tight.

4. Place the jars into canner with simmering water, ensuring that they are completely covered with water. Bring to a boil; process for 10 minutes. Remove jars and cool.

CHAMPAGNE JELLY

When I hosted a Christmas open house, each guest left with a jar of my blush-colored jelly. It was a hit! It's made with just pink champagne, sugar and fruit pectin.

—GAIL SHEPPARD SOMERVILLE, AL

PREP: 15 MIN. • **PROCESS:** 10 MIN.
MAKES: 3 HALF-PINTS

- **3 cups sugar**
- **2 cups pink champagne**
- **1 pouch (3 ounces) liquid fruit pectin**

1. In a Dutch oven, combine the sugar and champagne. Bring to a full rolling boil over high heat, stirring often. Stir in the pectin. Boil for 1 minute, stirring constantly.

2. Remove from the heat; skim off foam if necessary. Carefully ladle hot mixture into hot half-pint jars, leaving ¼-in. headspace. Wipe rims. Center lids on jars; screw on bands until fingertip tight.

3. Place the jars into canner with simmering water, ensuring that they are completely covered with water. Bring to a boil; process for 10 minutes. Remove jars and cool.

APPLE-WALNUT MAPLE CONSERVE

Versatile and delicious, this conserve reminds me of a warm cozy kitchen; you'll savor every bite. I warm the conserve and pour it over vanilla ice cream as a dessert, and it's great as a topping over French toast, biscuits or even pork roast. Be sure to make more than one batch so you can give it as gifts.
—PAULA MARCHESI LENHARTSVILLE, PA

PREP: 55 MIN. • **PROCESS:** 10 MIN.
MAKES: 11 HALF-PINTS

- 12 **cups chopped peeled Granny Smith apples (about 6 pounds)**
- 4 **cups sugar**
- 2 **cups packed brown sugar**
- 1 **cup maple syrup**
- 1 **teaspoon ground cinnamon**
- 1 **teaspoon pumpkin pie spice**
- 2 **cups finely chopped walnuts, toasted**

1. In a stockpot, combine apples, sugars, maple syrup, cinnamon and pie spice; bring to a boil. Cook, uncovered, 20-30 minutes or until apples are tender and mixture is slightly thickened. Stir in walnuts. Return to a boil; cook and stir 5 minutes longer.

2. Carefully ladle the hot mixture into 11 hot half-pint jars, leaving ¼-in. headspace. Remove air bubbles and adjust headspace, if necessary, by adding hot mixture. Wipe rims. Center lids on jars; screw on bands until fingertip tight.

3. Place jars into canner with simmering water, ensuring that they are completely covered with water. Bring to a boil; process for 10 minutes. Remove jars and cool.

NOTE *To toast nuts, spread in a 15x10x1-in. baking pan. Bake at 350° for 5-10 minutes or until lightly browned, stirring occasionally. Or, spread in a dry nonstick skillet and heat over low heat until lightly browned, stirring occasionally.*

PEAR & PINE NUT CONSERVE

This easy conserve pairs perfectly with grilled or roasted meats, and it's great as a flavorful topping for warm toast or pound cake. Sweet and savory...eating it is like taking my taste buds on a trip to Tuscany!

—SHANNON KOHN SIMPSONVILLE, SC

PREP: 1¼ HOURS • **PROCESS:** 10 MIN.
MAKES: 5 HALF-PINTS

- 1 **teaspoon olive oil**
- 1 **medium onion, chopped**
- 8 **cups chopped peeled ripe pears (about 10 medium)**
- 1½ **cups sugar**
- 2 **tablespoons grated orange peel**
- 2 **tablespoons orange juice**
- 1 **tablespoon minced fresh rosemary or 1 teaspoon dried rosemary, crushed**
- ¼ **cup coarsely chopped pine nuts, toasted**

1. In a Dutch oven, heat oil over medium heat. Add onion; cook and stir 6-8 minutes or until tender. Add pears, sugar, orange peel, orange juice and rosemary; bring to a boil. Reduce heat; simmer, uncovered, 40-45 minutes or until mixture is thickened, stirring occasionally. Stir in pine nuts. Return to a boil; cook and stir 5 minutes longer.

2. Carefully ladle hot mixture into five hot half-pint jars, leaving ¼-in. headspace. Remove air bubbles and adjust headspace, if necessary, by adding hot mixture. Wipe the rims. Center lids on jars; screw on bands until fingertip tight.

3. Place the jars into canner with simmering water, ensuring that they are completely covered with water. Bring to a boil; process for 10 minutes. Remove jars and cool.

RASPBERRY MINT JAM

I have so much mint growing in my yard that I like to add it to almost everything. What a revelation it was when it went in my raspberry jam the first time—the mint really wakes up the raspberry flavor.

—LAURIE BOCK LYNDEN, WA

PREP: 20 MIN.
PROCESS: 10 MIN.
MAKES: 8 HALF-PINTS

- 8 **cups fresh raspberries**
- 6½ **cups sugar**
- ½ **teaspoon butter**
- 2 **pouches (3 ounces each) liquid fruit pectin**
- 1 **cup minced fresh mint**

1. In a Dutch oven, combine the raspberries, sugar and butter. Bring to a full rolling boil over high heat, stirring constantly. Stir in pectin. Continue to boil 1 minute, stirring constantly.

2. Remove from heat; skim off foam. Stir in mint. Ladle hot mixture into eight hot half-pint jars, leaving ¼-in. headspace. Remove air bubbles and adjust headspace, if necessary, by adding hot mixture. Wipe the rims. Center lids on jars; screw on bands until fingertip tight.

3. Place the jars into canner with simmering water, ensuring that they are completely covered with water. Bring to a boil; process for 10 minutes. Remove jars and cool.

LEMON MARMALADE

Lemons and grapefruit combine to create a tantalizing spread for English muffins, toast and even shortbread cookies! I give away jars of this marmalade every Christmas.
—**BARBARA CARLUCCI** ORANGE PARK, FL

PREP: 40 MIN. • **PROCESS:** 10 MIN.
MAKES: 6 HALF-PINTS

- 3 **medium lemons**
- 1 **medium grapefruit**
- 4 **cups water**
- 1 **package (1¾ ounces) powdered fruit pectin**
- 4 **cups sugar**

1. Peel the rind from the lemons and grapefruit; cut into thin strips, about 1 in. long. Set aside fruit.

2. In a Dutch oven, combine water and citrus peel. Bring to a boil. Reduce heat; cover and simmer 5 minutes or until peel is softened. Remove from heat and set aside.

3. Trim white pith from reserved lemons and grapefruit; discard pith. Cut lemons and grapefruit into segments, discarding membranes and seeds. Chop pulp, reserving juices; stir into reserved peel mixture.

4. Add pectin. Bring to a full rolling boil over high heat, stirring constantly.

Stir in sugar; return to a full rolling boil. Boil and stir 1 minute.

5. Remove from heat; skim off foam. Ladle hot mixture into six hot half-pint jars, leaving ¼-in. headspace. Wipe the rims. Center lids on jars; screw on bands until fingertip tight.

6. Place the jars into canner with simmering water, ensuring that they are completely covered with water. Bring to a boil; process for 10 minutes. Remove jars and cool.

LIME MINT JELLY

PREP: 10 MIN. • **PROCESS:** 10 MIN.
MAKES: 5 HALF-PINTS

- 4 **cups sugar**
- 1¾ **cups water**
- ¾ **cup lime juice**
- 3 **to 4 drops green food coloring, optional**
- 1 **pouch (3 ounces) liquid fruit pectin**
- 3 **tablespoons finely chopped fresh mint leaves**
- ¼ **cup grated lime peel**

1. In a large saucepan, combine sugar, water and lime juice; if desired, add food coloring. Bring to a rolling boil over high heat, stirring constantly. Stir in pectin, mint and lime peel. Continue to boil 1 minute, stirring constantly.

2. Remove from heat; skim off foam. Ladle hot mixture into five hot half-pint jars, leaving ¼-in. headspace. Wipe the rims. Center lids on jars; screw on bands until fingertip tight.

3. Place the jars into canner with simmering water, ensuring that they are completely covered with water. Bring to a boil; process for 10 minutes. Remove jars and cool.

This bright green jelly won a Best of Show at the county fair and I was so thrilled. Flavored with lime, it's delicious on roasted meats. —**GLORIA JARRETT** LOVELAND, OH

STRAWBERRY-RHUBARB JAM

I consider this sweet flavorful jam summer in a jar! The fruity concoction is simply scrumptious. I even use it as a condiment for sandwiches.

—PEGGY WOODWARD EAST TROY, WI

PREP: 10 MIN. • **PROCESS:** 5 MIN.
MAKES: 6 PINTS

- 4 **cups fresh strawberries, crushed**
- 2 **cups chopped fresh rhubarb**
- ¼ **cup bottled lemon juice**
- 1 **package (1¾ ounces) powdered fruit pectin**
- 5½ **cups sugar**

1. In a Dutch oven, mix strawberries, rhubarb and lemon juice; stir in pectin. Bring to a full rolling boil, stirring constantly. Stir in sugar; return to a full rolling boil. Boil and stir 1 minute.

2. Remove from heat; skim off foam. Ladle hot mixture into six hot sterilized pint jars, leaving ¼-in. headspace. Remove air bubbles and adjust the headspace, if necessary, by adding hot mixture. Wipe rims. Center lids on jars; screw on bands until fingertip tight.

3. Place the jars into canner with simmering water, ensuring that they are completely covered with water. Bring to a boil; process for 5 minutes. Remove jars and cool.

DOUBLE-BERRY JALAPENO JAM

My friend and I had tried a fruity jam with jalapenos at a local vineyard and this is the version I created. At work there was a taste test comparing my different versions of the jam, and this one was voted the best. I like this fruity spread on crackers with cream cheese, on hamburgers or even grilled cheese. For extra heat, add the seeds of a few jalapenos to the jam.

—LISA KEIM WATERTOWN, NY

PREP: 15 MIN. • **PROCESS:** 10 MIN.
MAKES: 8 HALF-PINTS

- 2 **cups finely chopped seeded jalapeno pepper (about 1 pound)**
- 1½ **cups crushed strawberries (about 1 pound)**
- 1 **cup crushed blackberries (about ¾ pound)**
- 1 **package (1¾ ounces) powdered fruit pectin**
- 6⅔ **cups sugar**

1. In a large saucepan, combine jalapenos, strawberries and blackberries. Stir in pectin. Bring to a full rolling boil over high heat, stirring constantly. Stir in sugar; return to a full rolling boil. Boil and stir 1 minute.

2. Remove from heat; skim off foam. Ladle hot mixture into eight hot half-pint jars, leaving ¼-in. headspace. Remove air bubbles and adjust headspace, if necessary, by adding hot mixture. Wipe rims. Center lids on jars; screw on bands until fingertip tight.

3. Place jars into canner with simmering water, ensuring that they are completely covered with water. Bring to a boil; process for 10 minutes. Remove jars and cool.

NOTE *Wear disposable gloves when cutting hot peppers; the oils can burn skin. Avoid touching your face.*

CHUNKY CHERRY
& PEACH PRESERVES

Out of all the jams I make, this is my
grandmother's favorite. She anxiously waits
for June to come because she knows I'll
always bring home lots of peaches and
cherries so I can put up as many batches
as I can while the fruit is at its peak.
—AMY SEIGER MCLOUD, OK

PREP: 40 MIN. • **PROCESS:** 10 MIN.
MAKES: 7 HALF-PINTS

- 4 **cups chopped peeled fresh
  peaches (about 7 medium)**
- 4 **cups chopped pitted fresh tart
  cherries (about 2 pounds)**
- 2 **tablespoons lemon juice**
- 1 **package (1¾ ounces) pectin for
  lower sugar recipes**
- 3 **cups sugar**
- ¼ **teaspoon almond extract**

1. In a Dutch oven, combine peaches,
cherries and lemon juice; stir in pectin.
Bring to a full rolling boil over high
heat, stirring constantly. Stir in sugar;
return to a full rolling boil. Boil and
stir 1 minute.

2. Remove from heat; skim off foam.
Stir in extract. Ladle hot mixture into
seven hot half-pint jars, leaving ¼-in.
headspace. Remove air bubbles and
adjust headspace, if necessary, by
adding hot mixture. Wipe the rims.
Center lids on jars; screw on bands
until fingertip tight.

3. Place the jars into canner with
simmering water, ensuring that they
are completely covered with water.
Bring to a boil; process for 10 minutes.
Remove jars and cool.

GINGERBREAD SPICE JELLY

This jelly has won purple Champion ribbons at our County Fair two years in a row. I have made this simple jelly as gifts for many years and folks rave about how delicious it is. If only they knew how easy it is to prepare. People return my jelly jars to get them refilled every year.

—ROBIN NAGEL WHITEHALL, MT

PREP: 15 MIN. + STANDING
PROCESS: 10 MIN.
MAKES: 5 HALF-PINTS

- 2½ **cups water**
- 18 **gingerbread spice tea bags**
- 4½ **cups sugar**
- ½ **cup unsweetened apple juice**
- 2 **teaspoons butter**
- 2 **pouches (3 ounces each) liquid fruit pectin**

1. In a large saucepan, bring water to a boil. Remove from heat; add tea bags. Cover and steep 30 minutes.
2. Discard tea bags. Stir in the sugar, apple juice and butter. Bring to a full rolling boil over high heat, stirring constantly. Stir in pectin. Continue to boil 1 minute, stirring constantly.
3. Remove from heat; skim off foam. Ladle hot mixture into five hot half-pint jars, leaving ¼-in. headspace. Wipe the rims. Center lids on jars; screw on bands until fingertip tight.
4. Place the jars into canner with simmering water, ensuring that they are completely covered with water. Bring to a boil; process for 10 minutes. Remove jars and cool. (Jelly may take up to 2 weeks to set.)

This recipe makes ordinary orange marmalade into something really special! Sometimes I make it using strawberries that I've frozen without adding sugar or water. I just thaw them in the refrigerator overnight. —**MRS. CRAIG PRESBREY** PASCOAG, RI

STRAWBERRY MARMALADE

PREP: 1 HOUR • **PROCESS:** 10 MIN.
MAKES: 10 HALF-PINTS

- 2 **medium oranges**
- 2 **medium lemons**
- ½ **cup water**
- ⅛ **teaspoon baking soda**
- 1 **quart ripe strawberries, crushed**
- 7 **cups sugar**
- 1 **pouch (3 ounces) liquid fruit pectin**

1. Peel the outer layer of oranges and lemons; set aside. Remove the white membrane and seeds from fruit and discard. Set the fruit aside. Chop peels; place in a large saucepan. Add water and baking soda; cover and bring to a boil. Simmer for 10 minutes.

2. Section the oranges and lemons, reserving juice. Add fruit and juice to saucepan; cover and simmer for 20 minutes. Add strawberries. Measure fruit; return 4 cups to the saucepan. (If you have more than 4 cups, discard any extra; if less, add water to equal 4 cups.) Add sugar; mix well. Boil, uncovered, 5 minutes. Stir in pectin. Continue to boil 1 minute, stirring constantly.

3. Remove from heat; skim off foam. Carefully ladle into 10 hot half-pint jars, leaving ¼-in. headspace. Remove air bubbles and adjust headspace, if necessary, by adding hot mixture. Wipe the rims. Center lids on jars; screw on bands until fingertip tight.

4. Place the jars into canner with simmering water, ensuring that they are completely covered with water. Bring to a boil; process for 10 minutes. Remove jars and cool.

CHERRY ALMOND PRESERVES

My mother-in-law shared this preserve recipe with me. It's very old-fashioned—in fact, the friend who gave it to her used to cook it up on an old wood stove. With all the cherry orchards here in Bitterroot Valley, I make two batches each summer.
—**CONNIE LAWRENCE** HAMILTON, MT

PREP: 30 MIN. • **PROCESS:** 10 MIN.
MAKES: 11 HALF-PINTS

- 8 **cups pitted sour cherries (about 4 pounds)**
- 1½ **cups water**
- 10 **cups sugar**
- 2 **pouches (3 ounces each) liquid fruit pectin**
- 1 **teaspoon almond extract**

1. In a stockpot, bring cherries and water to a boil; boil 15 minutes.

2. Stir in sugar. Bring to a full rolling boil over high heat, stirring constantly. Boil 4 minutes. Stir in pectin. Continue to boil 1 minute, stirring constantly.

3. Remove from heat; skim off foam. Stir in extract. Ladle hot mixture into 11 hot half-pint jars, leaving ¼-in. headspace. Remove air bubbles and adjust headspace, if necessary, by adding hot mixture. Wipe rims. Center lids on jars; screw on bands until fingertip tight.

4. Place the jars into canner with simmering water, ensuring that they are completely covered with water. Bring to a boil; process for 10 minutes. Remove jars and cool.

APPLE PEAR &
WALNUT CONSERVE

Fruit and walnuts pair beautifully in this
homemade spread. It's wonderful on
pound cake and scoops of ice cream.

—GINNY BEADLE SPOKANE, WA

PREP: 30 MIN. • **PROCESS:** 10 MIN.
MAKES: 8 HALF-PINTS

- 4 **cups finely chopped peeled tart apples**
- 4 **cups finely chopped peeled ripe pears**
- 3 **clementines, peeled and chopped**
- ½ **cup lemon juice**
- 2 **packages (1¾ ounces each) powdered fruit pectin**
- 6 **cups sugar**
- ½ **teaspoon ground cinnamon**
- 1 **cup chopped walnuts, toasted**

1. In a Dutch oven over medium-high heat, bring apples, pears, clementines and lemon juice to a boil, stirring constantly. Reduce heat; simmer, uncovered, 10 minutes or until fruit is tender, stirring occasionally.

2. Stir in pectin. Bring to a full rolling boil over high heat, stirring constantly. Stir in sugar and cinnamon; return to bring to a full rolling boil. Boil and stir 1 minute.

3. Remove from heat; skim off foam. Stir in walnuts. Ladle hot mixture into eight hot half-pint jars, leaving ¼-in. headspace. Remove air bubbles and adjust headspace, if necessary, by adding hot mixture. Wipe the rims. Center lids on jars; screw on bands until fingertip tight.

4. Place the jars into canner with simmering water, ensuring that they are completely covered with water. Bring to a boil; process 10 minutes. Remove jars and cool.

CITRUS BLUEBERRY MARMALADE

I have four children under the age of six, so berry picking is the perfect family activity for us. I just started preserving fruit this season with all of the berries we picked—this is a spin-off of a super-easy recipe using ingredients we had on hand, with no added pectin, and it turned out fantastic. It's a favorite for kids and adults!

—SARAH HAENGEL BOWIE, MD

PREP: 1 HOUR • **PROCESS:** 10 MIN.
MAKES: 5 HALF-PINTS

- 4 **cups sugar**
- 2 **cups water**
- 1 **medium orange, quartered, thinly sliced and seeds removed**
- 1 **medium lemon, quartered, thinly sliced and seeds removed**
- 1 **medium lime, quartered, thinly sliced and seeds removed**
- 5 **cups fresh blueberries**

1. In a Dutch oven, combine sugar, water, orange, lemon and lime slices; bring to a boil. Reduce heat; simmer, uncovered, 15-20 minutes or until fruit is tender.

2. Add blueberries; increase heat to medium-high. Cook and stir 25-30 minutes or until slightly thickened.

3. Remove from heat; skim off foam. Ladle hot mixture into five hot half-pint jars, leaving 1/4-in. headspace. Remove air bubbles and adjust headspace, if necessary, by adding the hot mixture. Wipe rims. Center the lids on the jars; screw on bands until fingertip tight.

4. Place the jars into canner with simmering water, ensuring that they are completely covered with water. Bring to a boil; process for 10 minutes. Remove jars and cool.

CHERRY-RASPBERRY JAM

When sour cherries and raspberries are in season, I always freeze some with this recipe in mind. Friends and family agree this is the best jam I make.
—LENORA MCCULLEY REEDSVILLE, WI

PREP: 20 MIN. • **PROCESS:** 5 MIN.
MAKES: 8 HALF-PINTS

- 2½ cups finely chopped or ground sour cherries (about 1½ pounds)
- 2 cups red raspberries
- 1 package (1¾ ounces) powdered fruit pectin
- 5 cups sugar

1. In a Dutch oven, combine cherries and raspberries; stir in pectin. Bring to a full rolling boil over high heat, stirring constantly. Stir in sugar; return to a full rolling boil. Boil and stir 1 minute.
2. Remove from heat; skim off foam. Ladle hot mixture into eight hot sterilized half-pint jars, leaving ¼-in. headspace. Wipe the rims. Center lids on jars; screw on bands until fingertip tight.
3. Place the jars into canner with simmering water, ensuring that they are completely covered with water. Bring to a boil; process for 5 minutes. Remove jars and cool.

THREE-BERRY JAM

I sell many jars of this sweet berry jam at craft fairs. It's a wonderful way to preserve summer gems.
—BERNADETTE COLVIN TOMBALL, TX

PREP: 15 MIN.
PROCESS: 10 MIN.
MAKES: 9 PINTS AND 1 HALF-PINT

- 4 cups fresh blueberries
- 3 cups fresh strawberries
- 2 cups fresh raspberries
- ¼ cup bottled lemon juice
- 2 packages (1¾ ounces each) powdered fruit pectin
- 7 cups sugar

1. In a large saucepan, combine berries and lemon juice; crush slightly. Stir in pectin. Bring to a full rolling boil over high heat, stirring constantly. Stir in sugar; return to a full rolling boil. Boil and stir 1 minute.
2. Remove from the heat; skim off foam. Ladle hot mixture into nine hot 1-pint jars and one hot half-pint jar, leaving ¼-in. headspace. Remove air bubbles and adjust headspace, if necessary, by adding hot mixture. Wipe rims. Center lids on jars; screw on bands until fingertip tight.
3. Place the jars into canner with simmering water, ensuring that they are completely covered with water. Bring to a boil; process for 10 minutes. Remove jars and cool.

BLUEBERRY PRESERVES

Juicy blueberries swimming in a sweet jelly taste terrific spooned over vanilla ice cream. But we also enjoy it on top of waffles, French toast and pancakes at the breakfast table.

—SHANNON ARTHUR WHEELERSBURG, OH

PREP: 30 MIN. • **PROCESS:** 5 MIN.
MAKES: 3 HALF-PINTS

- 5 **cups fresh blueberries**
- 2¼ **cups sugar**
- 2 **teaspoons cider vinegar**
- ½ **teaspoon ground allspice**
- ½ **teaspoon ground cinnamon**
- ¼ **teaspoon ground cloves**

1. In a large saucepan, combine all ingredients. Bring to a boil; cook 15-18 minutes or until thickened, stirring frequently.

2. Remove from heat; skim off foam. Ladle hot mixture into three hot sterilized half-pint jars, leaving ¼-in. headspace. Remove air bubbles and adjust headspace, if necessary, by adding hot mixture. Wipe the rims. Center lids on jars; screw on bands until fingertip tight.

3. Place the jars into canner with simmering water, ensuring that they are completely covered with water. Bring to a boil; process 5 minutes. Remove jars and cool.

Any leftover blueberries after making jelly or jam will freeze beautifully. Place fresh berries on a baking sheet in your freezer for about 1½ hours or until frozen. Then, place in freezer bags. The berries won't stick together, so you can pour out any portion you desire.

I love the flavor combination of lemon and rosemary. This unique marmalade goes great with roast chicken, herbed pork roast, lamb chops or a savory biscuit. —**BIRDIE SHANNON** ARLINGTON, VA

LEMON-ROSEMARY MARMALADE

PREP: 2¼ HOURS • **PROCESS:** 10 MIN.
MAKES: 5 HALF-PINTS

- 7 **medium lemons (about 2 pounds)**
- ½ **teaspoon baking soda, divided**
- 7 **cups water**
- 4 **cups sugar**
- 4 **teaspoons minced fresh rosemary**
- 2 **drops yellow food coloring, optional**

1. Using a vegetable peeler, peel lemons into wide strips. With a sharp knife, carefully remove white pith from peels. Cut peels into ¼-in. strips. Set fruit aside.

2. Place lemon strips in a small saucepan; add water to cover and ¼ teaspoon baking soda. Bring to a boil. Reduce heat to medium. Cook, covered, 10 minutes; drain. Repeat with remaining baking soda.

3. Cut a thin slice from the top and bottom of lemons; stand lemons upright on a cutting board. With a knife, cut outer membrane from lemons. Working over a bowl to catch juices, cut along the membrane of each segment to remove fruit. Squeeze membrane to reserve additional juice.

4. Place lemon sections and reserved juices in a Dutch oven. Stir in 7 cups water and lemon peel. Bring to a boil. Reduce heat; simmer, uncovered, 25 minutes. Add sugar. Bring to a boil. Reduce heat; simmer, uncovered, 40-50 minutes or until slightly thickened, stirring occasionally. Remove from heat; immediately stir in rosemary and, if desired, food coloring.

5. Ladle hot mixture into five hot half-pint jars, leaving ¼-in. headspace. Wipe rims. Center lids on jars; screw on bands until fingertip tight.

6. Place the jars into canner with simmering water, ensuring that they are completely covered with water. Bring to a boil; process for 10 minutes. Remove jars and cool.

PEAR TOMATO PRESERVES

I have lived on a farm all my life, so I have always had a vegetable garden. I can a lot of my garden-grown produce and I make these wonderful preserves every year.
—EVELYN STEARNS ALTO PASS, IL

PREP: 1¼ HOURS • **PROCESS:** 20 MIN.
MAKES: 5 HALF-PINTS

- 4 **cups sugar**
- 1 **tablespoon ground cinnamon**
- 2 **teaspoons ground cloves**
- 1 **teaspoon ground ginger**
- 2 **medium lemons, chopped**
- 1 **cup water**
- 2 **pounds yellow pear tomatoes, chopped**

1. In a Dutch oven, combine sugar, spices, lemons and water. Cook over medium heat 15 minutes, stirring occasionally. Add tomatoes. Reduce heat to low; cook 45-60 minutes longer or until tomatoes become transparent, stirring frequently.

2. Ladle the hot mixture into five hot half-pint jars, leaving ¼-in. headspace. Remove air bubbles and adjust the headspace, if necessary, by adding hot mixture. Wipe rims. Center lids on jars; screw on bands until fingertip tight.

3. Place the jars into canner with simmering water, ensuring that they are completely covered with water. Bring to a boil; process 20 minutes. Remove jars and cool.

CHRISTMAS JAM

A few years ago, I hit upon the idea of presenting family and friends with baskets of homemade jam as gifts. With cherries, cinnamon and cloves, this smells and tastes exactly like Christmas!

—MARILYN REINEMAN STOCKTON, CA

PREP: 40 MIN. • **PROCESS:** 5 MIN.
MAKES: 12 HALF-PINTS

- **3** packages (12 ounces each) frozen pitted dark sweet cherries, thawed and coarsely chopped
- **2** cans (8 ounces each) unsweetened crushed pineapple, drained
- **1** package (12 ounces) frozen unsweetened raspberries, thawed
- **9** cups sugar
- **¼** cup lemon juice
- **¼** cup orange juice
- **¼** teaspoon ground cinnamon
- **¼** teaspoon ground cloves
- **¼** teaspoon butter
- **2** pouches (3 ounces each) liquid fruit pectin

1. In a Dutch oven, combine cherries, pineapple and raspberries. Stir in the sugar, juices, cinnamon, cloves and butter. Bring to a full rolling boil over high heat, stirring constantly. Stir in pectin. Continue to boil for 1 minute, stirring constantly.

2. Remove from heat; skim off foam. Ladle hot mixture into 12 hot sterilized half-pint jars, leaving ¼-in. headspace. Remove air bubbles and adjust headspace, if necessary, by adding hot mixture. Wipe rims. Center lids on jars; screw on bands until fingertip tight.

3. Place jars into canner with simmering water, ensuring that they are completely covered with water. Bring to a boil; process for 5 minutes. Remove jars and cool.

STRAWBERRY-THYME JAM

I created this recipe using two ingredients I love: strawberry and thyme. This recipe is ideal generously slathered on homemade farm biscuits or as a condiment for chicken.
—**SHARON DEMERS** DOLORES, CO

PREP: 25 MIN. • **PROCESS:** 10 MIN.
MAKES: 9 HALF-PINTS

- 5 **cups crushed strawberries (about 3 pounds)**
- ½ **teaspoon butter**
- 1 **package (1¾ ounces) powdered fruit pectin**
- 7 **cups sugar**
- 1 **tablespoon minced fresh thyme**

1. In a Dutch oven, combine the strawberries and butter. Stir in pectin. Bring to a full rolling boil over high heat, stirring constantly. Stir in sugar; return to a full rolling boil. Boil and stir for 1 minute. Immediately stir in thyme.

2. Remove from heat; skim off foam. Ladle hot mixture into nine hot half-pint jars, leaving ¼-in. headspace. Remove air bubbles; adjust headspace, if necessary, by adding hot mixture. Wipe rims. Center lids on jars; screw on bands until fingertip tight.

3. Place the jars into canner with simmering water, ensuring that they are completely covered. Bring to a boil; process for 10 minutes. Remove the jars and cool.

THREE-FRUIT MARMALADE

I make all my own jams, and this marmalade is a favorite. It marries the warm flavors of peaches and pears with citrus.

—LORRAINE WRIGHT GRAND FORKS, BC

PREP: 30 MIN. • **PROCESS:** 10 MIN.
MAKES: 8 HALF-PINTS

- 1 **medium orange**
- 2 **cups chopped peeled fresh peaches**
- 2 **cups chopped peeled fresh pears**
- 1 **package (1¾ ounces) powdered fruit pectin**
- 5 **cups sugar**

1. Finely grate peel from orange; peel and section the fruit. Place peel and sections in a Dutch oven. Add peaches and pears. Stir in pectin. Bring to a boil over high heat, stirring constantly. Stir in sugar; return to a full rolling boil. Boil and stir 1 minute.

2. Remove from heat; skim off foam. Ladle hot mixture into eight hot half-pint jars, leaving ¼-in. headspace. Remove the air bubbles and adjust headspace, if necessary, by adding hot mixture. Wipe rims. Center lids on jars; screw on bands until fingertip tight.

3. Place the jars into canner with simmering water, ensuring that they are completely covered with water. Bring to a boil; process for 10 minutes. Remove jars and cool.

STRAWBERRY BASIL JAM

I make this recipe with freshly picked strawberries and fresh basil grown in my own herb garden. This unique sweet and savory jam makes a perfect gift—just add a bright ribbon around the top with a gift tag!

—**JULIE O'NEIL** TWO HARBORS, MN

PREP: 25 MIN. • **PROCESS:** 10 MIN.
MAKES: 9 HALF-PINTS

- 5 **cups crushed strawberries (about 3 pounds)**
- 1 **teaspoon butter**
- 1 **package (1¾ ounces) powdered fruit pectin**
- 7 **cups sugar**
- ½ **cup minced fresh basil**

1. In a Dutch oven, combine the strawberries and butter. Stir in pectin. Bring to a full rolling boil over high heat, stirring constantly. Stir in sugar; return to a full rolling boil. Boil and stir 1 minute. Immediately stir in basil.

2. Remove from heat; skim off foam. Ladle the hot mixture into nine hot half-pint jars, leaving ¼-in. headspace. Remove the air bubbles and adjust headspace, if necessary, by adding hot mixture. Wipe rims. Center lids on jars; screw on bands until fingertip tight.

3. Place the jars into canner with simmering water, ensuring that they are completely covered with water. Bring to a boil; process for 10 minutes. Remove jars and cool.

TOMATO LEMON MARMALADE

This is a marmalade I make for our church bazaar every fall. It always sells out in no time at all.

—HELEN WITT MINNEAPOLIS, MN

PREP: 1¼ HOURS • **PROCESS:** 10 MIN.
MAKES: 9 HALF-PINTS

- 5 **medium ripe tomatoes**
- 4 **cups chopped peeled tart apples (about 4 large)**
- 2 **medium lemons, seeded and finely chopped**
- 6 **cups sugar**
- 2¼ **teaspoons ground ginger**
- 8 **whole cloves**

1. Peel, quarter and chop the tomatoes; place in a colander to drain. Transfer to a Dutch oven; add apples and lemons. Cook and stir over medium heat for 15 minutes. Add sugar and ginger. Tie cloves in a cheesecloth bag; add to the pot. Bring to a boil, stirring occasionally, and cook until sugar has dissolved. Reduce heat; simmer for 40 minutes, stirring frequently.

2. Remove spice bag. Carefully ladle hot mixture into nine hot half-pint jars, leaving ¼-in. headspace. Remove the air bubbles and adjust headspace, if necessary, by adding hot mixture. Wipe rims. Center lids on jars; screw on bands until fingertip tight.

3. Place the jars into canner with simmering water, ensuring that they are completely covered with water. Bring to a boil; process for 10 minutes. Remove jars and cool.

Peppers grow like wildfire during hot Missouri summers. That's when I make spicy jelly to give as gifts at Christmas. The leftover pulp can be frozen in small batches and stirred into chili, pasta sauce, salad dressing and salsa. —LEE BREMSON KANSAS CITY, MO

KICKIN' RED PEPPER JELLY

PREP: 30 MIN. • **PROCESS:** 10 MIN.
MAKES: 4 HALF-PINTS

- 5 medium sweet red peppers, coarsely chopped
- 3 jalapeno peppers, stemmed and seeded
- 2 garlic cloves, peeled
- ½ cup red wine vinegar
- 3 tablespoons balsamic vinegar
- 2 tablespoons bottled lemon juice
- 1 package (1¾ ounces) powdered fruit pectin
- 3¼ cups sugar

1. Place the red peppers, jalapenos and garlic in a blender; cover and process until finely chopped. Set aside ½ cup; puree the remaining pepper mixture.

2. Line a strainer with four layers of cheesecloth and place over a bowl. Place the pureed pepper mixture in strainer; cover with edges of the cheesecloth. Let stand 30 minutes or until liquid measures 1½ cups.

3. Discard pepper pulp puree from cheesecloth or save for another use; place liquid in a large saucepan. Stir in vinegars, lemon juice, pectin and reserved pepper mixture. Bring to a full rolling boil over high heat, stirring constantly. Stir in sugar; return to a full rolling boil. Boil stir 1 minute.

4. Remove from heat; skim off foam. Ladle hot mixture into four hot half-pint jars, leaving ¼-in. headspace. Wipe rims. Center lids on jars; screw on bands until fingertip tight.

5. Place jars into canner with simmering water, ensuring that they are completely covered with water. Bring to a boil; process for 10 minutes. Remove jars and cool.

NOTE *When cutting hot peppers, disposable gloves are recommended. The oils can burn skin. Avoid touching your face.*

CARAMELIZED ONION JAM

This savory jam is very good served with meats—we especially like it with venison.

—VANESSA LAMBERT SIOUX FALLS, SD

PREP: 50 MIN. • **PROCESS:** 10 MIN.
MAKES: ABOUT 3½ PINTS

- 4 **whole garlic bulbs**
- 1 **teaspoon canola oil**
- 5 **cups chopped sweet onions (1½ pounds)**
- ¼ **cup butter, cubed**
- ¾ **cup cider vinegar**
- ½ **cup bottled lemon juice**
- ¼ **cup balsamic vinegar**
- 1½ **teaspoons ground mustard**
- 1 **teaspoon salt**
- ¾ **teaspoon white pepper**
- ½ **teaspoon ground ginger**
- ¼ **teaspoon ground cloves**
- 6 **cups sugar**
- 1 **pouch (3 ounces) liquid fruit pectin**

1. Preheat oven to 425°. Remove papery outer skin from garlic (do not peel or separate cloves). Cut top off garlic bulbs; brush with oil. Wrap each bulb in heavy-duty foil. Bake 30-35 minutes or until softened. Cool 10-15 minutes.

2. In a Dutch oven, saute the onions in butter 30-40 minutes or until lightly browned. Squeeze softened garlic into pan. Stir in cider vinegar, lemon juice, balsamic vinegar, mustard, salt, pepper, ginger and cloves. Bring to a full rolling boil over high heat, stirring constantly. Gradually stir in sugar. Return to a boil; boil 3 minutes. Stir in pectin. Continue to boil 1 minute, stirring constantly.

3. Remove from heat; let stand for 3 minutes. Skim off foam. Ladle hot mixture into three hot half-pint jars, leaving ¼-in. headspace. Remove air bubbles and adjust the headspace, if necessary, by adding hot mixture. Wipe rims. Center lids on jars; screw on bands until fingertip tight.

4. Place the jars into canner with simmering water, ensuring that they are completely covered with water. Bring to a boil; process for 10 minutes. Remove jars and cool.

APRICOT RHUBARB CONSERVE

My conserve is great on toast, but it also makes an exceptional sweetener for my tea.

—LAURAE FORTNER-WELCH BIG LAKE, AK

PREP: 30 MIN. • **PROCESS:** 10 MIN.
MAKES: 7 HALF-PINTS

- 8 **ounces dried apricots, finely chopped**
- 6 **cups sugar**
- 4 **cups chopped fresh or frozen rhubarb, thawed and undrained**
- ½ **cup chopped orange pulp and peel**
- ½ **cup chopped lemon pulp and peel**
- ½ **cup chopped walnuts**

1. Place apricots in a bowl and cover with water; soak overnight. Drain and place in a Dutch oven. Add sugar, rhubarb, orange and lemon. Cook over medium heat until a candy thermometer reads 220°, stirring frequently. Stir in walnuts.

2. Carefully ladle hot mixture into seven hot half-pint jars, leaving ¼-in. headspace. Remove air bubbles and adjust headspace, if necessary, by adding hot mixture. Wipe rims. Center lids on jars; screw on bands until fingertip tight.

3. Place jars into canner with simmering water, ensuring that they are completely covered with water. Bring to a boil; process 10 minutes. Remove jars and cool.

APRICOT HABANERO JAM

I warm this jam and brush it over a baking pork roast. It has a spicy-sweet taste that appeals to all my dinner guests.
—**MEGAN TAYLOR** GREENFIELD, WI

PREP: 15 MIN. • **PROCESS:** 10 MIN.
MAKES: 11 HALF-PINTS

- 3½ **pounds fresh apricots**
- 6 **tablespoons bottled lemon juice**
- 2 **to 4 habanero peppers, seeded**
- 1 **package (1¾ ounces) powdered fruit pectin**
- 7 **cups sugar**

1. Pit and chop apricots; place in a Dutch oven or stockpot. Stir in lemon juice. Place habaneros in a blender; add a small amount of apricot mixture. Cover and process until smooth. Return to the pan. Stir in pectin. Bring to a full rolling boil over high heat, stirring constantly. Stir in sugar; return to a full rolling boil. Boil and stir 1 minute.

2. Remove from heat; skim off foam. Pour hot mixture into 11 hot sterilized jars, leaving ¼-in. headspace. Remove air bubbles and adjust headspace, if necessary, by adding hot mixture. Wipe rims. Center lids on jars; screw on bands until fingertip tight.

3. Place the jars into canner with simmering water, ensuring that they are completely covered with water. Bring to a boil; process for 10 minutes. Remove jars and cool. For best results, let processed jam stand at room temperature for 2 weeks to set up.

NOTE *When cutting hot peppers, disposable gloves are recommended. The oils can burn skin. Avoid touching your face.*

APPLE PIE JAM

My husband and I love this jam so much because it tastes just like apple pie without the crust!

—AUDREY GODELL STANTON, MI

PREP: 30 MIN. • **PROCESS:** 10 MIN.
MAKES: 7 HALF-PINTS

- **4** **to 5 large Golden Delicious apples, peeled and sliced (about 2 pounds)**
- **1** **cup water**
- **5** **cups sugar**
- **½** **teaspoon butter**
- **1** **pouch (3 ounces) liquid fruit pectin**
- **1½** **teaspoons ground cinnamon**
- **1** **teaspoon ground nutmeg**
- **¼** **teaspoon ground mace, optional**

1. In a Dutch oven, combine apples and water. Cover and cook slowly until tender. Measure 4½ cups apples; return to the pan. (Save remaining apple mixture for another use or discard.)

2. Stir in sugar and butter. Bring to a full rolling boil over high heat, stirring constantly. Stir in pectin. Continue to boil 1 minute, stirring constantly.

3. Remove from heat; skim off foam. Stir in spices. Carefully ladle the hot mixture into seven hot half-pint jars, leaving ¼-in. headspace. Remove the air bubbles and adjust headspace, if necessary, by adding hot mixture. Wipe rims. Center lids on jars; screw on bands until fingertip tight.

4. Place the jars into canner with simmering water, ensuring that they are completely covered with water. Bring to a boil; process 10 minutes. Remove jars and cool.

RHUBARB MARMALADE

When rhubarb is abundant in the spring, my daughter heads to her kitchen to make this marmalade. Our family enjoys her gift...a refreshing departure in flavor from all the berry jams and jellies.

—LEO NERBONNE DELTA JUCTION, AK

PREP: 1¼ HOURS • **PROCESS:** 10 MIN.
MAKES: ABOUT 8 HALF-PINTS

- **6 cups chopped fresh or frozen rhubarb**
- **6 cups sugar**
- **2 medium oranges**

1. Combine rhubarb and sugar in a Dutch oven. Grind oranges, including the peels, in a food processor; add to rhubarb mixture. Bring to a boil.

Reduce heat and simmer, uncovered, stirring often until marmalade sheets from a spoon, about 1 hour.

2. Remove from heat; skim off foam. Ladle the hot mixture into eight hot half-pint jars, leaving ¼-in. headspace. Remove the air bubbles and adjust headspace, if necessary, by adding hot mixture. Wipe rims. Center lids on jars; screw on bands until fingertip tight.

3. Place the jars into canner with simmering water, ensuring that they are completely covered with water. Bring to a boil; process for 10 minutes. Remove jars and cool.

NOTE *If using frozen rhubarb, measure rhubarb while still frozen, then thaw completely. Drain in a colander, but do not press liquid out.*

POMEGRANATE JELLY

For as long as I can remember, my mom has been preparing pomegranate jelly and sending us all home with a few jars. To make this jelly even more tangy, try substituting cranberry juice for pomegranate juice.

—TATIANA HENDRICKS VISALIA, CA

PREP: 15 MIN. • **PROCESS:** 5 MIN.
MAKES: 6 HALF-PINTS

- 3½ **cups pomegranate juice**
- 1 **package (1¾ ounces) powdered fruit pectin**
- 5 **cups sugar**

1. In a Dutch oven, combine the pomegranate juice and pectin. Bring to a full rolling boil over high heat, stirring constantly. Stir in sugar; return to a full rolling boil. Boil and stir 2 minutes.

2. Remove from heat; skim off foam. Ladle hot liquid into six hot sterilized half-pint jars, leaving ¼-in. headspace. Wipe rims. Center lids on jars; screw on bands until fingertip tight.

3. Place the jars into canner with simmering water, ensuring that they are completely covered with water. Bring to a boil; process for 5 minutes. Remove jars and cool.

RASPBERRY PLUM JAM

PREP: 25 MIN. • **PROCESS:** 10 MIN.
MAKES: 6 PINTS

- 4½ cups chopped or coarsely ground peeled pitted fresh plums (2½ pounds)
- 2 packages (10 ounces each) frozen sweetened raspberries
- 10 cups sugar
- ½ cup bottled lemon juice
- 2 pouches (3 ounces each) liquid fruit pectin

1. In a Dutch oven, combine the plums, raspberries, sugar and lemon juice. Bring to a full rolling boil over high heat, stirring constantly. Stir in the pectin. Continue to boil 1 minute, stirring constantly.

2. Remove from heat; skim off foam. Ladle hot mixture into six hot 1-pint jars, leaving ¼-in. headspace. Remove air bubbles and adjust headspace, if necessary, by adding hot mixture. Wipe rims. Center lids on jars; screw on bands until fingertip tight.

3. Place the jars into canner with simmering water, ensuring that they are completely covered with water. Bring to a boil; process for 10 minutes. Remove jars and cool.

> The thing I like best about this jam is the way the plums stretch the flavor of the raspberries. I make it when plums are in season, and we enjoy it all winter long.
> **—ARLENE LOKER** CRAIGVILLE, IN

PEAR PRESERVES

In the fall we would go to our farm and pick pears and apples. Then we'd build a campfire and roast hot dogs. Later we'd all get together and make big batches of these tasty preserves.
—TAMMY WATKINS GREENTOP, MO

PREP: 2 HOURS • **PROCESS:** 10 MIN.
MAKES: 7 HALF-PINTS

- 16 cups peeled, sliced fresh pears (about 16 medium)
- 4 cups sugar
- 2 cups water
- 3 tablespoons lemon juice

1. In a stockpot, combine pears, sugar, water and lemon juice; bring to a boil. Cook, uncovered, 1½ to 2 hours or until mixture reaches a thick, spreadable consistency.

2. Remove from heat. Ladle hot mixture into seven hot half-pint jars, leaving ¼-in. headspace. Remove air bubbles and adjust headspace, if necessary, by adding hot mixture. Wipe rims. Center lids on jars; screw on bands until fingertip tight.

3. Place the jars into canner with simmering water, ensuring that they are completely covered with water. Bring to a boil; process for 10 minutes. Remove jars and cool.

JALAPENO PEPPER JELLY

My family relishes this jelly served with meat or spread on crackers with cream cheese.
—**BEV ELLIOTT** PEOTONE, IL

PREP: 30 MIN. • **PROCESS:** 10 MIN.
MAKES: 5 HALF-PINTS

- 5 **cups sugar**
- 2 **medium tart apples, peeled and coarsely chopped**
- 1½ **cups cider vinegar**
- ¾ **cup finely chopped green pepper**
- 8 **to 10 jalapeno peppers, seeded and chopped**
- ¼ **cup water**
- 6 **to 8 drops green food coloring**
- 2 **pouches (3 ounces each) liquid fruit pectin**
  Cream cheese and assorted crackers

1. In a large saucepan, combine sugar, apples, vinegar, green pepper, jalapenos and water. Bring to a boil. Reduce heat; simmer, uncovered, 10 minutes. Strain mixture and return to pan. Stir in food coloring. Bring to a full rolling boil over high heat, stirring constantly. Stir in pectin. Continue to boil 1 minute, stirring constantly.

2. Remove from heat; skim off foam. Ladle hot mixture into five hot half-pint jars, leaving ¼-in. headspace. Wipe the rims. Center lids on jars; screw on bands until fingertip tight.

3. Place the jars into canner with simmering water, ensuring that they are completely covered with water. Bring to a boil; process for 10 minutes. Remove jars and cool. Serve with cream cheese on crackers.

NOTE *Wear disposable gloves when cutting hot peppers; the oils can burn skin. Avoid touching your face.*

CARAMEL APPLE JAM

I created this recipe one year when I had excess apples. The brown sugar gives the jam a wonderful caramel taste. I'm a retired master baker and cook who really enjoys preparing Southern dishes for my wife of 48 years, two sons and five grandchildren.

—ROBERT ATWOOD WEST WAREHAM, MA

PREP: 30 MIN. • **PROCESS:** 10 MIN.
MAKES: 7 HALF-PINTS

- **6 cups diced peeled apples (⅛-inch cubes)**
- **½ cup water**
- **½ teaspoon butter**
- **½ teaspoon ground cinnamon**
- **¼ teaspoon ground nutmeg**
- **1 package (1¾ ounces) powdered fruit pectin**
- **3 cups sugar**
- **2 cups packed brown sugar**

1. In a Dutch oven, combine the apples, water, butter, cinnamon and nutmeg. Cook and stir over low heat until apples are tender. Stir in pectin. Bring to a full rolling boil over high heat, stirring constantly. Stir in sugar; return to a full rolling boil. Boil and stir 1 minute.

2. Remove from heat; skim off foam. Ladle the hot mixture into seven hot half-pint jars, leaving ¼-in. headspace. Remove the air bubbles and adjust headspace, if necessary, by adding hot mixture. Wipe rims. Center lids on jars; screw on bands until fingertip tight.

3. Place the jars into canner with simmering water, ensuring that they are completely covered with water. Bring to a boil; process for 10 minutes. Remove jars and cool.

AMARETTO-PEACH PRESERVES

Chock-full of peaches, raisins and pecans, this is a lovely conserve your family will love.

—REDAWNA KALYNCHUK BARRHEAD, AB

PREP: 1¼ HOURS • **PROCESS:** 10 MIN.
MAKES: 5 HALF-PINTS

- **1 cup golden raisins**
- **¾ cup boiling water**
- **2 pounds peaches, peeled and chopped**
- **4 teaspoons grated orange peel**
- **⅓ cup orange juice**
- **2 tablespoons lemon juice**
- **3 cups sugar**
- **½ cup chopped pecans**
- **3 tablespoons amaretto**

1. Place raisins in a bowl. Cover with boiling water; let stand 5 minutes. Place raisins with liquid in a large saucepan.

Add peaches and orange peel. Bring to a boil. Reduce heat. Cover; simmer 10-15 minutes or until peaches are tender.

2. Stir in orange and lemon juices; return to a boil. Add sugar. Cook, uncovered, over medium heat for 25-30 minutes or until thickened, stirring occasionally. Add pecans; cook 5 minutes longer. Remove from heat; stir in amaretto.

3. Carefully ladle hot mixture into five hot sterilized half-pint jars, leaving ¼-in. headspace. Remove air bubbles and adjust headspace, if necessary, by adding hot mixture. Wipe rims. Center lids on jars; screw on the bands until fingertip tight.

4. Place the jars into canner with simmering water, ensuring that they are completely covered with water. Bring to a boil; process for 5 minutes. Remove jars and cool.

PLUM ORANGE JAM

We put our homegrown plums to delicious use in this quick and easy jam. It's my favorite thing to serve with biscuits.
—**KATHY RAIRIGH** MILFORD, IN

PREP: 30 MIN. • **PROCESS:** 5 MIN.
MAKES: 10 HALF-PINTS

- 10 **cups chopped plums (about 4½ pounds)**
- 1 **cup orange juice**
- 1 **package (1¾ ounces) pectin for lower sugar recipes**
- 3 **cups sugar**
- 3 **tablespoons grated orange peel**
- 1½ **teaspoons ground cinnamon**

1. In a Dutch oven, combine plums and orange juice; bring to a boil. Reduce heat; simmer, covered, 5-7 minutes or until softened, stirring occasionally. Stir in pectin. Bring to a full rolling boil over high heat, stirring constantly. Stir in sugar; return to a full rolling boil. Boil and stir 1 minute.

2. Remove from heat; skim off foam. Ladle hot mixture into 10 hot sterilized half-pint jars, leaving ¼-in. headspace. Remove the air bubbles and adjust headspace, if necessary, by adding hot mixture. Wipe rims. Center lids on jars; screw on bands until fingertip tight.

3. Place the jars into canner with simmering water, ensuring that they are completely covered with water. Bring to a boil; process for 5 minutes. Remove jars and cool.

Pickles, Relishes & Salsas

The processing times listed for all the recipes in this chapter are for altitudes of 1,000 feet or less. For altitudes up to 3,000 feet, add 5 minutes; 6,000 feet, add 10 minutes; 8,000 feet, add 15 minutes; 10,000 feet, add 20 minutes.

FAVORITE BREAD & BUTTER PICKLES

I made these pickles when I was growing up and loved them because they go with just about anything. Today, my children adore the pickles, too. I think you'll enjoy them as much as we do!

—LINDA WEGER ROBINSON, IL

PREP: 45 MIN. + STANDING • **PROCESS:** 10 MIN.
MAKES: 11 PINTS

- 20 **cups sliced cucumbers (about 12 medium)**
- 3 **cups sliced onions (about 4 medium)**
- 1 **medium sweet red pepper, sliced**
- 1 **medium green pepper, sliced**
- 3 **quarts ice water**
- ½ **cup canning salt**
- 6 **cups sugar**
- 6 **cups white vinegar**
- 3 **tablespoons mustard seed**
- 3 **teaspoons celery seed**
- 1½ **teaspoons ground turmeric**
- ¼ **teaspoon plus ⅛ teaspoon ground cloves**

1. Place cucumbers, onions and peppers in a large bowl. In another large bowl, mix ice water and salt; pour over vegetables. Let stand 3 hours.

2. Rinse vegetables and drain well. Pack the vegetables into 11 hot 1-pint jars to within ½ in. of the top.

3. In a Dutch oven, bring sugar, vinegar, mustard seed, celery seed, turmeric and cloves to a boil. Carefully ladle hot liquid over vegetable mixture, leaving ½-in. headspace. Remove air bubbles and adjust headspace, if necessary, by adding hot liquid. Wipe rims. Center lids on jars; screw on bands until fingertip tight.

4. Place jars into canner, ensuring that they are completely covered with water. Bring to a boil; process for 10 minutes. Remove jars and cool.

within 1/2 in. of top. Place one dill head, two garlic cloves and two peppers in each jar.

2. Carefully ladle hot mixture into jars, leaving 1/2-in. headspace. Remove any air bubbles and adjust headspace, if necessary, by adding hot mixture. Wipe rims. Center lids on jars; screw on bands until fingertip tight.

3. Place the jars into canner with simmering water, ensuring that they are completely covered with water. Bring to a boil; process for 15 minutes. Remove jars and cool.

TANGY PICKLED MUSHROOMS

PREP: 50 MIN. • **PROCESS:** 20 MIN.
MAKES: 8 PINTS

- 5 **pounds small fresh mushrooms**
- 2 **large onions, halved and sliced**
- 2 **cups white vinegar**
- 1½ **cups canola oil**
- ¼ **cup sugar**
- 2 **tablespoons canning salt**
- 3 **garlic cloves, minced**
- 1½ **teaspoons pepper**
- ¼ **teaspoon dried tarragon**

1. Place all ingredients in a stockpot. Bring to a boil. Reduce heat; simmer, uncovered, 10 minutes. Carefully ladle hot mixture into eight hot 1-pint jars, leaving 1/2-in. headspace.

2. Remove air bubbles and adjust headspace, if necessary, by adding hot mixture. Wipe rims. Center lids on jars; screw on bands until fingertip tight.

3. Place the jars into canner with simmering water, ensuring that they are completely covered with water. Bring to a boil; process for 20 minutes. Remove jars and cool.

GRANDMA'S DILL PICKLES

Treasured family recipes become like old friends. These crispy spears have a slightly salty, tart flavor.

—BETTY KAY SITZMAN WRAY, CO

PREP: 50 MIN. • **PROCESS:** 15 MIN.
MAKES: 9 QUARTS

- 11 **cups water**
- 5 **cups white vinegar**
- 1 **cup canning salt**
- 12 **pounds pickling cucumbers, quartered or halved lengthwise**
- 9 **dill sprigs or heads**
- 18 **garlic cloves**
- 18 **dried hot chilies**

1. In a stockpot, bring water, vinegar and salt to a boil; boil 10 minutes. Pack cucumbers into nine hot quart jars

Home-canned pickled mushrooms are a great addition to your pantry. They're wonderful for cocktails, appetizers, salads and relish trays.
—**JILL HIHN** WEST GROVE, PA

IOWA CORN RELISH

I've been making colorful corn relish for more than 30 years, and my family never tires of it. It's excellent served with roasted turkey, pork or ham.

—DEANNA OGLE BELLINGHAM, WA

PREP: 1 HOUR • **PROCESS:** 20 MIN.
MAKES: 5 PINTS

- 20 **medium ears sweet corn**
- 2⅔ **cups white vinegar**
- 2 **cups water**
- 1½ **cups sugar**
- 2 **medium onions, chopped**
- 2 **celery ribs, chopped**
- 1 **large green pepper, chopped**
- 1 **large sweet red pepper, chopped**
- 4½ **teaspoons mustard seed**
- 1 **tablespoon canning salt**
- 1 **teaspoon celery seed**
- ½ **teaspoon ground turmeric**

1. Place corn in a stockpot; cover with water. Bring to a boil; cover and cook 3 minutes or until tender. Drain. Cut corn from cobs, making about 10 cups. Return corn to the pan; add remaining ingredients. Bring to a boil. Reduce heat and simmer 20 minutes.

2. Carefully ladle hot mixture into five hot 1-pint jars, leaving ½-in. headspace. Remove the air bubbles and adjust headspace, if necessary, by adding hot mixture. Wipe rims. Center lids on jars; screw on bands until fingertip tight.

3. Place jars into canner with simmering water, ensuring that they are completely covered with water. Bring to a boil; process for 20 minutes. Remove jars and cool.

PICKLED SWEET ONIONS

These slightly crunchy pickled onions are not only a great gift for Christmas, but also a terrific contribution to a backyard barbecue as a condiment for burgers and hot dogs.

—LAURA WINEMILLER DELTA, PA

PREP: 30 MIN. + STANDING
PROCESS: 10 MIN. • **MAKES:** 4 HALF-PINTS

- **8 cups thinly sliced sweet onions**
- **2 tablespoons canning salt**
- **1¾ cups white vinegar**
- **1 cup sugar**
- **1 teaspoon dried thyme**

1. Place onions in a colander over a plate; sprinkle with canning salt and toss. Let stand 1 hour. Rinse and drain onions, squeezing to remove excess liquid.

2. In a Dutch oven, combine vinegar, sugar and thyme; bring to a boil. Add onions and return to a boil. Reduce heat; simmer, uncovered, 10 minutes. Remove from heat.

3. Carefully ladle hot mixture into four hot half-pint jars, leaving ½-in. headspace. Remove air bubbles and adjust headspace, if necessary, by adding hot mixture. Wipe rims. Center lids on jars; screw on bands until fingertip tight.

4. Place the jars into canner with simmering water, ensuring that they are completely covered with water. Bring to a boil; process for 10 minutes. Remove jars and cool. Refrigerate remaining relish up to 1 week.

CANDIED JALAPENOS & GARLIC

If you love spicy food, then these tasty jalapenos and garlic bits are for you! The sweet and spicy favorite is great over sandwiches, burgers and cream cheese , or try it with nachos or right out of the jar—if you dare, that is!

—RITA LADANY EDISON, NJ

PREP: 25 MIN. • **PROCESS:** 15 MIN.
MAKES: 3 PINTS

- 1 **pound jalapeno peppers (about 16), cut into ¼-inch slices**
- 1½ **cups thinly sliced garlic cloves (about 4 bulbs)**
- 3½ **cups sugar**
- 1¼ **cups red wine vinegar**
- ¾ **teaspoon salt**
- ¾ **teaspoon mustard seed**
- ¾ **teaspoon celery seed**
- ½ **teaspoon ground turmeric**
- 1 **cayenne pepper, minced, optional**

1. Pack jalapenos and garlic into three hot 1-pint jars to within ½ in. of the top. In a large saucepan, bring sugar, vinegar, seasonings and, if desired, cayenne pepper to a boil. Reduce heat; simmer, uncovered, 5 minutes.
2. Carefully ladle hot liquid over pepper mixture, leaving ½-in. headspace. Remove the air bubbles and adjust headspace, if necessary, by adding hot mixture. Wipe rims. Center lids on jars; screw on bands until fingertip tight.
3. Place the jars into canner with simmering water, ensuring that they are completely covered with water. Bring to a boil; process for 15 minutes. Remove jars and cool.
NOTE *Wear disposable gloves with cutting hot peppers; the oils can burn skin. Avoid touching your face.*

YELLOW SUMMER SQUASH RELISH

My friends can barely wait for the growing season to arrive so I can make my incredible relish. Its color really dresses up a hot dog.

—**RUTH HAWKINS** JACKSON, MS

PREP: 1 HOUR + MARINATING • **PROCESS:** 15 MIN.
MAKES: 6 PINTS

- 10 **cups shredded yellow summer squash (about 4 pounds)**
- 2 **large onions, chopped**
- 1 **large green pepper, chopped**
- 6 **tablespoons canning salt**
- 4 **cups sugar**
- 3 **cups cider vinegar**
- 1 **tablespoon each celery seed, ground mustard and ground turmeric**
- ½ **teaspoon ground nutmeg**
- ½ **teaspoon pepper**

1. In a large container, combine squash, onions, green pepper and salt. Cover and refrigerate overnight. Drain; rinse and drain again.

2. In a Dutch oven, combine sugar, vinegar and seasonings; bring to a boil. Add squash mixture; return to a boil. Reduce heat; simmer 15 minutes. Remove from heat.

3. Carefully ladle hot mixture into six hot 1-pint jars, leaving ½-in. headspace. Remove the air bubbles and adjust headspace, if necessary, by adding hot mixture. Wipe rims. Center lids on jars; screw on bands until fingertip tight.

4. Place jars into canner with simmering water, ensuring that they are completely covered with water. Bring to a boil; process for 15 minutes. Remove jars and cool. Refrigerate remaining relish up to 1 week.

MILD TOMATO SALSA

PREP: 1½ HOURS • **PROCESS:** 20 MIN.
MAKES: 10 PINTS

- 36 medium tomatoes, peeled and quartered
- 4 medium green peppers, chopped
- 3 large onions, chopped
- 2 cans (12 ounces each) tomato paste
- 1¾ cups white vinegar
- ½ cup sugar
- 1 medium sweet red pepper, chopped
- 1 celery rib, chopped
- 15 garlic cloves, minced
- 4 to 5 jalapeno peppers, seeded and chopped
- ¼ cup canning salt
- ¼ to ½ teaspoon hot pepper sauce

1. In a large stockpot, cook the tomatoes, uncovered, over medium heat 20 minutes. Drain, reserving 2 cups liquid. Return tomatoes to the pot.

2. Stir in green peppers, onions, tomato paste, vinegar, sugar, red pepper, celery, garlic, jalapenos, canning salt, hot pepper sauce and the reserved tomato liquid. Bring to a boil. Reduce heat; simmer, uncovered, 1 hour, stirring frequently.

3. Ladle hot mixture into 10 hot 1-pint jars, leaving ½-in. headspace. Remove air bubbles and adjust headspace, if necessary, by adding hot mixture. Wipe rims. Center lids on jars; screw on bands until fingertip tight.

4. Place the jars into canner with simmering water, ensuring that they are completely covered with water. Bring to a boil; process for 20 minutes. Remove jars and cool.

NOTE *Wear disposable gloves when cutting hot peppers; the oils can burn skin. Avoid touching your face.*

After my sister gave me her salsa recipe, we had to try it right away. My children and I have been making batches of it ever since. We pair pint jars with packages of tortilla chips for neighborly gifts.
—**PAMELA LUNDSTRUM**
BIRD ISLAND, MN

WATERMELON RIND PICKLES

"Waste not, want not" has always been smart advice—especially when it produces results that are so refreshing.

—*TASTE OF HOME* TEST KITCHEN

PREP: 45 MIN. + CHILLING
PROCESS: 10 MIN. • **MAKES:** 4 PINTS

- **8 cups sliced peeled watermelon rind (2x1-inch pieces)**
- **6 cups water**
- **1 cup canning salt**
- **4 cups sugar**
- **2 cups white vinegar**
- **6 cinnamon sticks (3 inches), divided**
- **1 teaspoon whole cloves**
- **1 teaspoon whole peppercorns**

1. Place rind in a large nonreactive bowl; stir in water and salt. Refrigerate for several hours or overnight. Rinse and drain well.

2. In a Dutch oven, mix the sugar, vinegar, 2 cinnamon sticks, cloves and peppercorns. Bring to a boil. Add rinds; return to a boil. Reduce heat; simmer, uncovered, 10 minutes or until tender. Discard cinnamon sticks.

3. Carefully ladle hot mixture into four hot 1-pint jars, leaving 1/2-in. headspace. Add a remaining cinnamon stick to each jar. Remove air bubbles and adjust headspace, if necessary, by adding hot mixture. Wipe rims. Center lids on jars; screw on bands until fingertip tight.

4. Place the jars into canner with simmering water, ensuring that they are completely covered with water. Bring to a boil; process for 10 minutes. Remove jars and cool.

NOTE *To prepare watermelon rind, remove dark green peel from watermelon rind and discard.*

GIARDINIERA

Sweet and tangy, this Italian condiment is packed with peppers, cauliflower, carrots and other crisp-tender veggies. It's perfect to offer alongside pickles or olives on a relish tray.

—TASTE OF HOME TEST KITCHEN

PREP: 1 HOUR • **PROCESS:** 10 MIN.
MAKES: 10 PINTS

- 6   **cups white vinegar**
- 3½ **cups sugar**
- 3   **cups water**
- 4½ **teaspoons canning salt**
- 1   **tablespoon dried oregano**
- 1   **tablespoon fennel seed**
- 2   **small heads cauliflower, broken into small florets (about 12 cups)**
- 4   **large carrots, sliced**
- 4   **celery ribs, cut into ½-inch slices**
- 48 **pearl onions, peeled and trimmed (about 1¼ pounds)**
- 4   **large sweet red peppers, cut into ½-inch strips**
- 4   **serrano peppers, seeds removed and thinly sliced**
- 10 **bay leaves**
- 20 **whole peppercorns**
- 10 **garlic cloves, thinly sliced**

1. In a large stockpot, combine vinegar, sugar, water, canning salt, oregano and fennel seed. Bring to a boil. Add the cauliflower, carrots, celery, and onions; return to a boil. Remove from heat; add the peppers.

2. Carefully ladle the hot mixture into 10 hot 1-pint jars, leaving ½- in. headspace. To each jar, add a bay leaf, 2 peppercorns and a few slices of garlic. Remove the air bubbles and adjust headspace, if necessary, by adding hot mixture. Wipe rims. Center lids on jars; screw on bands until fingertip tight.

3. Place the jars into canner with simmering water, ensuring that they are completely covered with water. Bring to a boil; process for 10 minutes. Remove jars and cool.

NOTE *Wear disposable gloves when cutting hot peppers; the oils can burn skin. Avoid touching your face.*

FOOD TRIVIA!

Giardiniera is a traditional Italian mixture of pickled vegetables. It can vary from mild to hot or as Chicagoans like it— extremely hot! Depending on the size of the veggies, it can be used in salads or antipasto, as a side dish or a sandwich topping, especially on Italian beef.

_____
_____
_____
_____
_____
_____
_____
_____
_____
_____
_____
_____
_____
_____
_____
_____
_____
_____
_____
_____
_____
_____
_____
_____
_____
_____
_____
_____
_____
_____
_____
_____

PINEAPPLE SALSA

Here's a sweet and spicy twist on salsa. Served with chips, it's an excellent party starter. It also adds a refreshing touch to grilled fish or meat.
—ANGELA LONGTIN CAVALIER, ND

PREP: 50 MIN. • **PROCESS:** 15 MIN.
MAKES: 7 PINT JARS

- 12 **medium tomatoes (about 4 pounds)**
- 2 **large red onions, chopped**
- 2 **medium green peppers, chopped**
- 2 **cans (8 ounces each) unsweetened crushed pineapple, drained**
- 1 **can (15 ounces) tomato sauce**
- 1 **can (12 ounces) tomato paste**
- 3 **cans (4 ounces each) chopped green chilies**
- 2 **cans (4 ounces each) diced jalapeno peppers, drained**
- ⅓ **cup white vinegar**
- 2 **tablespoons salt**
- 6 **garlic cloves, minced**
- 2 **teaspoons ground cumin**
- 1 **teaspoon pepper**

1. In a large saucepan, bring 8 cups water to a boil. Add tomatoes, a few at a time; boil for 30 seconds. Drain and immediately place tomatoes in ice water. Drain and pat dry; peel and chop.

2. In a stockpot, combine remaining ingredients. Stir in tomatoes. Bring to a boil over medium-high heat. Reduce heat; simmer, uncovered, 15-20 minutes or to desired thickness.

3. Carefully ladle hot mixture into seven hot 1-pint jars, leaving ½-in. headspace. Remove air bubbles and adjust headspace, if necessary, by adding hot mixture. Wipe rims. Center lids on jars; screw on bands until fingertip tight.

4. Place jars into canner with simmering water, ensuring that they are completely covered with water. Bring to a boil; process for 15 minutes. Remove jars and cool.

SWEET & SPICY PICKLED RED SEEDLESS GRAPES

Most people don't think about grapes when creating a canned pickle recipe. Here, the pickling liquid includes red wine, vinegar and common pickling spices as well as warm spices such as cinnamon and star anise. The flavor-packed bites are delicious on an antipasto, pickle or cheese tray.

—CHERYL PERRY HERTFORD, NC

PREP: 35 MIN. • **PROCESS:** 10 MIN.
MAKES: 4 PINTS

- 5 **cups seedless red grapes**
- 4 **jalapeno peppers, seeded and sliced**
- 2 **tablespoons minced fresh gingerroot**
- 2 **cinnamon sticks (3 inches), halved**
- 4 **whole star anise**
- 2 **teaspoons coriander seeds**
- 2 **teaspoons mustard seed**
- 2 **cups packed brown sugar**
- 2 **cups white wine vinegar**
- 1 **cup water**
- 1 **cup dry red wine**
- 1½ **teaspoons canning salt**

1. Pack grapes into four hot 1-pint jars to within 1½ in. of the top. Divide the jalapenos, ginger, cinnamon, star anise, coriander seeds and mustard seed among jars.

2. In a large saucepan, combine brown sugar, vinegar, water, wine and canning salt. Bring to a boil; cook 15-18 minutes or until liquid is reduced to 3 cups.

3. Carefully ladle hot liquid over grape mixture, leaving ½-in. headspace. Remove the air bubbles and adjust headspace, if necessary, by adding hot liquid. Wipe rims. Center lids on jars; screw on bands until fingertip tight.

4. Place jars into canner, ensuring that they are completely covered with water. Bring to a boil; process for 10 minutes. Remove jars and cool.

NOTE *Wear disposable gloves when cutting hot peppers; the oils can burn skin. Avoid touching your face.*

PICKLED SWEET PEPPERS

I'm nearing the age of 80 and still love to can my homegrown produce. This recipe feels like summer in a jar. The peppers have a nice combination of tart and spicy flavors.
—**EDNA CLEMENS** WEST BRANCH, MI

PREP: 30 MIN. • **PROCESS:** 15 MIN.
MAKES: 5 PINTS

5	large sweet red peppers
8	banana peppers (about 1 pound)
1	medium onion, thinly sliced
8	garlic cloves, peeled
4	teaspoons canola oil
2½	cups water
2½	cups white vinegar
1¼	cups sugar
2	teaspoons canning salt

1. Cut red and banana peppers into strips, discarding seeds. Pack peppers into five hot 1-pint jars to within ½ in. of the top. Divide the onion, garlic and oil among jars.

2. In a large saucepan, bring water, vinegar, sugar and salt to a boil. Carefully ladle hot liquid over pepper mixture, leaving ½-in. headspace. Remove the air bubbles and adjust headspace, if necessary, by adding hot liquid. Wipe rims. Center lids on jars; screw on bands until fingertip tight.

3. Place the jars into canner with simmering water, ensuring that they are completely covered with water. Bring to a boil; process for 15 minutes. Remove jars and cool.

AUTUMN PEPPER RELISH

My vibrant peppers and fruit condiment is a favorite with friends and family—everyone always asks for the recipe because it tastes great on just about everything. I like to serve it over cream cheese or a block of sharp cheddar cheese along with crackers or a sliced French baguette.

—BARBARA PLETZKE HERNDON, VA

PREP: 1 HOUR 20 MIN. + STANDING
PROCESS: 20 MIN. • **MAKES:** 8 HALF-PINTS

- 8 **medium sweet red peppers (about 3 pounds)**
- 6 **jalapeno peppers**
- 4 **medium Granny Smith apples (about 1¼ pounds)**
- 2 **medium pears (about 1 pound)**
- 1 **medium onion**
- 3 **tablespoons canning salt**
- 2 **cups white vinegar**
- 2 **cups sugar**
- 1 **cup packed brown sugar**
- ¾ **teaspoon fennel seed**

1. Seed and coarsely chop peppers. Peel and cut apples, pears and onion into 1-in. pieces. Pulse in batches in a food processor until finely chopped. Transfer to a large bowl; sprinkle with salt and toss. Let stand for 6 hours. Rinse and drain well; blot dry with paper towels.

2. In a Dutch oven, combine drained pepper mixture, vinegar, sugars and fennel seed; bring to a boil. Reduce heat; simmer, uncovered, 40-45 minutes or until slightly thickened.

3. Carefully ladle hot mixture into eight hot half-pint jars, leaving ½-in. headspace. Remove the air bubbles and adjust headspace, if necessary, by adding hot mixture. Wipe rims. Center lids on jars; screw on bands until fingertip tight.

4. Place the jars into canner with simmering water, ensuring that they are completely covered with water. Bring to a boil; process for 20 minutes. Remove jars and cool.

NOTE *Wear disposable gloves when cutting hot peppers; the oils can burn skin. Avoid touching your face.*

PICKLED GREEN BEANS

This recipe produces zippy little pickles and preserves my green beans for months to come—if they even last that long. I crank up the heat a bit with cayenne pepper.

—MARISA MCCLELLAN PHILADELPHIA, PA

PREP: 20 MIN. • **PROCESS:** 10 MIN.
MAKES: 4 PINTS

- 1¾ **pounds fresh green beans, trimmed**
- 1 **teaspoon cayenne pepper**
- 4 **garlic cloves, peeled**
- 4 **teaspoons dill seed or 4 fresh dill heads**
- 2½ **cups water**
- 2½ **cups white vinegar**
- ¼ **cup canning salt**

1. Pack beans into four hot 1-pint jars to within ½ in. of the top. Add cayenne, garlic and dill seed to jars.

2. In a large saucepan, bring water, vinegar and salt to a boil.

3. Carefully ladle hot liquid over beans, leaving ½-in. headspace. Remove the air bubbles and adjust headspace, if necessary, by adding the hot mixture. Wipe rims. Center lids on jars; screw on bands until fingertip tight.

4. Place the jars into canner with simmering water, ensuring that they are completely covered with water. Bring to a boil; process for 10 minutes. Remove jars and cool.

SWEET & SMOKY SALSA

I love the roasted flavor that grilling gives food, so I decided to make a salsa from grilled vegetables. If you can't use wood chip charcoal, you might try adding a little liquid smoke to the salsa while it cooks.

—SHELLY BEVINGTON HERMISTON, OR

PREP: 1 HOUR • **PROCESS:** 15 MIN.
MAKES: 4 PINTS

- 1 **cup soaked mesquite wood chips**
- 2 **medium onions**
- 12 **garlic cloves, peeled**
- 3 **teaspoons barbecue seasoning, divided**
- 2 **pounds tomatillos, husks removed (about 12)**
- 2 **pounds plum tomatoes (about 8)**
- 6 **jalapeno peppers**
- 1½ **cups cider vinegar**
- 1¼ **cups packed brown sugar**
- 1½ **teaspoons salt**
- ½ **teaspoon pepper**
- ⅓ **cup minced fresh cilantro**

1. Add wood chips to grill according to manufacturer's directions. Moisten a paper towel with cooking oil; using long-handled tongs, rub on grill rack and grilling grid to coat lightly.

2. Cut the onions in quarters; place in a small bowl. Add the garlic and

1½ teaspoons barbecue seasoning; toss to coat. Arrange on grilling grid; place on grill rack. Grill, covered, over medium heat 10-15 minutes or until tender, turning occasionally.

3. Meanwhile, cut tomatillos, tomatoes and jalapenos in half; place in a large bowl. Add the remaining barbecue seasoning; toss to coat. Grill in batches, covered, over medium heat 4-6 minutes or until tender, turning occasionally.

4. When cool enough to handle, chop vegetables. Transfer to a Dutch oven; stir in vinegar, brown sugar, salt and pepper. Bring to a boil. Reduce heat; simmer, uncovered, 15-20 minutes or until slightly thickened. Stir in cilantro.

5. Carefully ladle hot mixture into four hot 1-pint jars, leaving ½-in. headspace. Remove the air bubbles and adjust headspace, if necessary, by adding hot mixture. Wipe rims. Center lids on jars; screw on bands until fingertip tight.

6. Place the jars into canner with simmering water, ensuring that they are completely covered with water. Bring to a boil; process for 15 minutes. Remove jars and cool.

NOTE *Wear disposable gloves when cutting hot peppers; the oils can burn skin. Avoid touching your face.*

GARDEN'S HARVEST PICKLES

This relish recipe I received from a friend is similar to giardiniera but sweeter.

—LINDA CHAPMAN MERIDEN, IA

PREP: 1 HOUR + CHILLING
PROCESS: 20 MIN.
MAKES: 11 PINTS

- 3 **large onions, cut into wedges**
- 3 **medium green peppers, cut into 1-inch pieces**

3 medium sweet red peppers, cut into 1-inch pieces
¼ cup canning salt
6 celery ribs, cut into 2-inch lengths
6 medium carrots, cut into ½-inch slices
3 cups cauliflower florets
3 cups cut fresh green beans (2-inch lengths)
3 medium zucchini, cut into 1-inch slices
6 cups sugar
6 cups white vinegar
¼ cup mustard seed
¼ cup celery seed

1. In a bowl, mix first four ingredients. Cover and refrigerate overnight.
2. Drain; place in a stockpot. Add the remaining ingredients. Bring to a boil. Reduce heat; simmer, uncovered, 15-20 minutes or until tender. Carefully ladle into 11 hot 1-pint jars, leaving ½-in. headspace. Remove air bubbles and adjust headspace, if necessary, by adding hot mixture. Wipe rims. Center lids on jars; screw on bands until fingertip tight.
3. Place the jars into canner with simmering water, ensuring that they are completely covered with water. Bring to a boil; process for 20 minutes. Remove jars and cool.

SPICY PICKLED GARLIC

Here's a delectable condiment for the garlic lover on your list. You'll be pleasantly surprised how pickling mellows out the garlic, making it a tasty sandwich topper.
—*TASTE OF HOME* TEST KITCHEN

PREP: 20 MIN. • **PROCESS:** 10 MIN.
MAKES: 3 HALF-PINTS

2 quarts water
3 cups peeled garlic cloves

12 coriander seeds
6 whole peppercorns
3 dried hot chilies, split
3 whole allspice
1 bay leaf, torn into three pieces
1½ cups white wine vinegar or distilled white vinegar
1 tablespoon sugar
1½ teaspoons canning salt

1. In a large saucepan, bring water to a boil. Add garlic and boil 1 minute.
2. Meanwhile, divide coriander, peppercorns, chilies, allspice and bay leaf among three hot half-pint jars. Drain garlic and pack into jars to within ½ in. of the top.
3. In a small saucepan, combine the vinegar, sugar and salt. Bring to a boil, stirring constantly. Carefully ladle hot liquid over garlic, leaving ½-in. headspace. Remove air bubbles and adjust headspace, if necessary, by adding hot mixture. Wipe rims. Center lids on jars; screw on bands until fingertip tight.
4. Place the jars into canner with simmering water, ensuring that they are completely covered with water. Bring to a boil; process for 10 minutes. Remove jars and cool.

SWEET PICKLED ASPARAGUS

Here in Washington, we enjoy lots of fresh asparagus in the spring. This is how my grandmother used to pickle it.
—**VALERIE GIESBRECHT** OTHELLO, WA

PREP: 15 MIN.
PROCESS: 20 MIN.
MAKES: 5 QUARTS

- 10 **pounds fresh asparagus**
- 5 **tablespoons dill seed**
- 5 **teaspoons mixed pickling spices**
- 2 **quarts water**
- 3 **cups cider vinegar**
- ⅔ **cup sugar**
- ¼ **cup canning salt**

1. Wash, drain and trim asparagus; cut into 5¾-in. spears (discard ends or save for another use). Pack the asparagus into five 1-quart jars to within ½ in. of top. Place 1 tablespoon dill seed and 1 teaspoon pickling spices in each jar.
2. In a Dutch oven, bring water, vinegar, sugar and salt to a boil. Carefully ladle hot liquid over asparagus mixture, leaving ½-in. headspace. Remove air bubbles and adjust headspace, if necessary, by adding hot mixture. Wipe rims. Center lids on jars; screw on bands until fingertip tight.
3. Place jars into canner with simmering water, ensuring that they are completely covered with water. Bring to a boil; process for 15 minutes. Remove jars and cool.

JERK-SPICED MANGO PINEAPPLE CHUTNEY

PREP: 1½ HOURS • **PROCESS:** 10 MIN.
MAKES: 5 HALF-PINTS

- 4 **cups chopped peeled ripe mangoes (about 4 medium)**
- 4 **cups finely chopped fresh pineapple**
- 2½ **cups packed brown sugar**
- 1½ **cups cider vinegar**
- 1 **large onion, chopped**
- ⅓ **cup finely chopped crystallized ginger**
- 1 **Scotch bonnet or habanero pepper, seeded and minced**
- 2 **tablespoons minced fresh thyme or 2 teaspoons dried thyme**
- 2 **tablespoons rum**
- 2 **garlic cloves, minced**
- 2 **teaspoons ground allspice**
- 1 **teaspoon ground cinnamon**

1. In a Dutch oven, bring all the ingredients to a boil. Reduce heat; simmer, uncovered, 1 to 1¼ hours or until thickened.
2. Carefully ladle hot mixture into five hot half-pint jars, leaving ½-in. headspace. Remove air bubbles and adjust headspace, if necessary, by adding hot mixture. Wipe rims. Center lids on jars; screw on the bands until fingertip tight.
3. Place the jars into canner with simmering water, ensuring that they are completely covered with water. Bring to a boil; process for 10 minutes. Remove jars and cool.
NOTE *Wear disposable gloves when cutting hot peppers; the oils can burn skin. Avoid touching your face.*

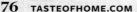

I grew up eating mango, pineapple and spicy food, so I really enjoy the blend of these flavors. Adjust the spiciness to suit your taste buds. The chutney is delish with meat or fish.
—SUGIYARTI JORGENSON KODIAK, AK

PICKLED BRUSSELS SPROUTS

When I asked my brother what he wanted for his birthday, he said, "pickled Brussels sprouts." While I was not familiar with them, it's hard for me to say "no" to my brother. He got his wish and we both thought the Brussels sprouts were delicious!

—**HEATHER KING** FROSTBURG, MD

PREP: 30 MIN. • **PROCESS:** 10 MIN.
MAKES: 6 PINTS

- 3 **pounds fresh Brussels sprouts, trimmed and halved (about 12 cups)**
- 6 **garlic cloves, halved**
- 2 **teaspoons crushed red pepper flakes**
- 2½ **cups water**
- 2½ **cups white vinegar**
- 1 **medium onion, thinly sliced**
- 1 **medium sweet red pepper, finely chopped**
- ½ **cup sugar**
- 3 **tablespoons canning salt**
- 1 **tablespoon celery seed**
- 1 **tablespoon whole peppercorns**

1. Fill a Dutch oven three-fourths full with water; bring to a boil. Add Brussels sprouts in batches; cook, uncovered, 4 minutes or until crisp-tender. Remove with a slotted spoon and immediately drop into ice water. Drain and pat dry.

2. Pack Brussels sprouts into six hot 1-pint jars. Divide garlic and pepper flakes among jars.

3. In a large saucepan, bring remaining ingredients to a boil. Carefully ladle hot liquid over Brussels sprouts, leaving ½-in. headspace. Remove air bubbles and adjust headspace, if necessary, by adding hot mixture. Wipe rims. Center lids on jars; screw on the bands until fingertip tight.

4. Place the jars into canner with simmering water, ensuring that they are completely covered with water. Bring to a boil; process for 10 minutes. Remove jars and cool.

TOMATILLO RELISH

I have a very hearty tomatillo plant in my garden. To use up the abundant produce, I make this relish every year.
—DEB LABOSCO FOLEY, MN

PREP: 45 MIN. • **PROCESS:** 20 MIN.
MAKES: 4 PINTS

- 1 **pound tomatillos, husks removed, quartered**
- 1 **pound plum tomatoes, quartered**
- 2 **medium green peppers, seeded and quartered**
- 1 **medium sweet red pepper, seeded and quartered**
- 4 **jalapeno peppers, seeded**
- 1 **large onion, quartered**
- 1 **whole garlic bulb, separated into cloves**
- ¼ **cup fresh cilantro leaves**
- ¼ **cup packed fresh parsley sprigs**
- ½ **cup olive oil**
- ½ **cup cider vinegar**
- 1 **can (2¼ ounces) sliced ripe olives, drained**
- 4 **teaspoons canning salt**
- 1½ **teaspoons pepper**
- ¼ **teaspoon crushed red pepper flakes**
- 4 **tablespoons bottled lemon juice**

1. In a food processor, process first nine ingredients in batches until chopped.
2. Transfer to a large stockpot; stir in oil, vinegar, olives, salt, pepper and pepper flakes. Bring to a boil. Reduce heat; cover and simmer 20 minutes or until vegetables are tender.

3. Add lemon juice to four hot pint jars, 1 tablespoon in each. Ladle hot mixture into jars, leaving ½-in. headspace. Remove any air bubbles and adjust headspace, if necessary, by adding hot mixture. Wipe rims. Center lids on jars; screw on bands until fingertip tight.
4. Place the jars into canner with simmering water, ensuring that they are completely covered with water. Bring to a boil; process for 20 minutes. Remove jars and cool.
NOTE *Wear disposable gloves when cutting hot peppers; the oils can burn skin. Avoid touching your face.*

FOOD TRIVIA!
Tomatillo is also called a Mexican green tomato.
Tomatillos are mild in flavor and offer a hint of lemon and apple which is enhanced by cooking.

JALAPENO BREAD & BUTTER PICKLES

Even people with tastebuds sensitive to spice will want to dip into these bread and butter pickles that pack a surprising wallop. *Ay caramba!* They're fantastic!
—**KAREN OWEN** RISING SUN, IN

PREP: 45 MIN. + STANDING • **PROCESS:** 15 MIN.
MAKES: 7 PINTS

- 4 **pounds cucumbers, sliced**
- 5 **small onions, sliced**
- 4 **jalapeno peppers, sliced and seeded**
- ½ **cup canning salt**
- 5 **cups sugar**
- 4 **cups white vinegar**
- 2 **tablespoons mustard seed**
- 2 **teaspoons celery seed**
- 1½ **teaspoons ground turmeric**
- ½ **teaspoon ground cloves**

1. In a large container, combine the cucumbers, onions, jalapenos and salt. Cover with crushed ice and mix well. Let stand 3 hours. Drain; rinse and drain again.

2. In a Dutch oven, combine sugar, vinegar and seasonings; bring to a boil. Add cucumber mixture; return to a boil. Remove from heat.

3. Carefully ladle hot mixture into seven hot 1-pint jars, leaving ½-in. headspace. Remove air bubbles and adjust headspace, if necessary, by adding hot mixture. Wipe rims. Center lids on jars; screw on bands until fingertip tight.

4. Place jars into canner with simmering water, ensuring that they are completely covered with water. Bring to a boil; process for 15 minutes. Remove jars and cool.

NOTE *Wear disposable gloves when cutting hot peppers; the oils can burn skin. Avoid touching your face.*

SPICED PICKLED BEETS

With sweet, tangy and spiced flavors, these pickled beets are so good, they'll convert any and all naysayers!

—EDNA HOFFMAN HEBRON, IN

PREP: 1¼ HOURS • **PROCESS:** 35 MIN.
MAKES: 4 PINTS

- 3 **pounds small fresh beets**
- 2 **cups sugar**
- 2 **cups water**
- 2 **cups cider vinegar**
- 2 **cinnamon sticks (3 inches)**
- 1 **teaspoon whole cloves**
- 1 **teaspoon whole allspice**

1. Scrub beets and trim tops to 1 in. Place in a Dutch oven and cover with water. Bring to a boil. Reduce heat; cover and simmer 25-35 minutes or until tender. Remove from water; cool. Peel beets and cut into fourths.

2. Place beets in a Dutch oven. Add sugar, water and vinegar. Place spices on a double thickness of cheesecloth; bring up corners of cloth and tie with string to form a bag. Add to the beet mixture. Bring to a boil. Reduce heat; cover and simmer 10 minutes. Discard spice bag.

3. Carefully pack beets into four hot 1-pint jars to within ½ in. of the top. Carefully ladle hot liquid over beets, leaving ½-in. headspace. Remove the air bubbles and adjust headspace, if necessary, by adding hot mixture. Wipe rims. Center lids on jars; screw on bands until fingertip tight.

4. Place the jars into canner with simmering water, ensuring that they are completely covered with water. Bring to a boil; process for 35 minutes. Remove jars and cool.

When I'm left with green tomatoes at the end of summer, I reach for this recipe. Friends and family are so happy to receive the sweet-sour relish that they often return the empty jar and ask for a refill!

—**MARY GILL** FLORENCE, OR

Sweet peppers are also referred to as bell pepper because they are shaped like a bell. Sweet red peppers are actually green peppers that have been left to ripen on the vine until they turn red. Due to their extra time on the vine, sweet red peppers are indeed sweeter than green peppers.

PICKLED GREEN TOMATO RELISH

PREP: 1 HOUR + STANDING
PROCESS: 15 MIN. • **MAKES:** 8 PINTS

- **7 pounds green tomatoes (about 20 medium)**
- **4 large onions**
- **2 large red onions**
- **3 large green peppers**
- **2 large sweet red peppers**
- **4 teaspoons canning salt**
- **5 cups cider vinegar**
- **4 cups sugar**
- **2 tablespoons celery seed**
- **4 teaspoons mustard seed**

1. Cut tomatoes, onions and peppers into wedges. In a food processor, cover and process vegetables in batches until finely chopped. Stir in salt. Divide mixture between two strainers and place each over a bowl. Let stand 3 hours.

2. Discard liquid from bowls. Place vegetables in a stockpot; stir in vinegar, sugar, celery seed and mustard seed. Bring to a boil. Reduce heat; simmer, uncovered, 30-35 minutes or until thickened.

3. Carefully ladle hot mixture into eight hot 1-pint jars, leaving 1/2-in. headspace. Remove the air bubbles and adjust headspace, if necessary, by adding hot mixture. Wipe rims. Center lids on jars; screw on the bands until fingertip tight.

4. Place the jars into canner with simmering water, ensuring that they are completely covered with water. Bring to a boil; process for 15 minutes. Remove jars and cool.

PICKLED ZUCCHINI SLICES

Here's a great way to put your garden bounty to good use! Turn that ripe zucchini into a crunchy, flavorful burger topping.
—**ROMAINE WETZEL** RONKS, PA

PREP: 35 MIN. + STANDING
PROCESS: 10 MIN. • **MAKES:** 5 PINTS

- **8 cups sliced zucchini**
- **4 large onions, sliced**
- **1 large green pepper, sliced**
- **3 tablespoons canning salt**
- **1 quart white vinegar**
- **2 cups sugar**
- **2 teaspoons celery salt**
- **2 teaspoons ground turmeric**
- **1 teaspoon ground mustard**

1. In a large bowl, combine zucchini, onions and pepper; sprinkle with canning salt and cover with cold water. Let stand 2 hours; rinse and drain.

2. In a large saucepan, bring remaining ingredients to a boil. Pour over zucchini mixture; cover and let stand 2 hours.

3. Transfer to a stockpot. Bring to a boil. Reduce heat; simmer, uncovered, 5 minutes.

4. Carefully ladle hot mixture into five hot 1-pint jars, leaving 1/2-in. headspace. Remove the air bubbles and adjust headspace, if necessary, by adding hot mixture. Wipe rims. Center lids on jars; screw on bands until fingertip tight.

5. Place the jars into canner with simmering water, ensuring that they are completely covered with water. Bring to a boil; process for 10 minutes. Remove jars and cool.

Freezer & Fridge Faves

QUINCE ORANGE MARMALADE

Quince sweetens this marmalade as it simmers and fills the house with its distinctive autumn aroma.

—TASTE OF HOME TEST KITCHEN

PREP: 30 MIN. • **COOK:** 1½ HOURS + CHILLING
MAKES: 3 CUPS

- 5 **cups chopped peeled quince (about 4 medium)**
- 1½ **cups water**
- 1⅓ **cups sugar**
- 1 **cup orange juice**
- 1 **tablespoon grated orange peel**

1. Rinse three 1-cup plastic containers and lids with boiling water. Dry thoroughly

2. In a large saucepan, bring all ingredients to a boil. Reduce heat; simmer, uncovered, 1½ to 1¾ hours or until mixture is reduced to 3 cups; stir frequently. Cool slightly; carefully mash. Fill all containers to within ½ in. of tops. Wipe off top edges. Cool to room temperature. Refrigerate up to 3 weeks or freeze up to 1 year. Thaw frozen marmalade in refrigerator before serving.

DILLED ONION RELISH

Dads will enjoy these treats. Serve the relish with dinner or give as a gift he can truly savor.

—DONNA TORRES GRAND RAPIDS, MN

PREP: 20 MIN. + STANDING • **MAKES:** 2 CUPS

- 2 **large sweet onions, cut into ¼-inch slices**
- 1 **teaspoon dill seed**
- ½ **cup sugar**
- ½ **cup white vinegar**
- ¼ **cup water**
- 2 **teaspoons salt**

Sprinkle the onions with dill seed. Layer in a wide-mouth pint jar. In a saucepan, cook and stir remaining ingredients over medium heat until sugar is dissolved. Pour over onions. Refrigerate in an airtight container 36 hours. Serve as a relish .

CHERRY RHUBARB JAM

This tangy-sweet spread is jam-packed with lots of cherry flavor, plus a hint of rhubarb. My mother gives jars of it to friends during rhubarb season.

—FAYE SAMPSON RADCLIFFE, IA

PREP: 10 MIN. + STANDING
COOK: 15 MIN. + COOLING
MAKES: 5 CUPS

- **4 cups diced fresh or frozen rhubarb**
- **1½ cups sugar**
- **1 package (3 ounces) cherry gelatin**
- **1 can (21 ounces) cherry pie filling**
- **⅛ teaspoon almond extract, optional**

1. In a large saucepan, combine the rhubarb and sugar; let stand for 1½ hours, stirring occasionally.

2. Bring to a boil; cook, uncovered, 10 minutes or until rhubarb is tender. Remove from heat; stir in gelatin until dissolved. Stir in pie filling and extract if desired.

3. Immediately fill containers to within ½ in. of tops. Wipe off top edges of containers. Cool completely before covering. Refrigerate up to 3 weeks.

PICKLED BELL PEPPERS

Everyone around here knows me for this colorful, tasty dish. I serve the peppers with a lot of meals. Sometime I'll turn it into a salad for a weeknight cookout.

—HEATHER PRENDERGAST
SUNDRE, ALBERTA

PREP: 20 MIN. + CHILLING • **YIELD:** 4 CUPS

- **2 each medium green, sweet red and yellow peppers, cut into 1-inch pieces**
- **1 large red onion, halved and thinly sliced**
- **2 teaspoons mixed pickling spices**
- **½ teaspoon celery seed**
- **1 cup sugar**
- **1 cup cider vinegar**
- **⅓ cup water**

1. In a large glass bowl, combine the peppers and onion. Place the pickling spices and celery seed on a double thickness of cheesecloth. Gather the corners of cloth to enclose seasonings; tie securely with string.

2. In a small saucepan, combine sugar, vinegar, water and spice bag. Bring to a boil; boil 1 minute. Transfer spice bag to pepper mixture. Pour vinegar mixture over top. Cool to room temperature. Refrigerate, covered, for 24 hours, stirring occasionally.

3. Discard spice bag. Refrigerate pickled peppers up to 1 month.

CRISP SWEET PICKLES

My mom's delicious pickles, a Christmas tradition, are quick and easy to make since they start with a jar of purchased dill pickles and then are just dressed up. They would make a nice gift in a pretty glass jar.

—**DENISE BITNER** REEDSVILLE, PA

PREP: 10 MIN. + CHILLING
MAKES: 1 QUART

- 1 jar (32 ounces) whole kosher dill pickle slices, drained
- 1¼ cups sugar
- 3 tablespoons cider vinegar
- 1 tablespoon dried minced onion
- 1 tablespoon celery seed

Cut the pickles into ½-in. slices; return the slicese to the jar. Add the remaining ingredients. Cover and shake until coated. Refrigerate at least 1 week, shaking the jar occasionally. Serve pickles with a slotted spoon.

BREAD & BUTTER PEPPERS

PREP: 20 MIN. + STANDING
COOK: 5 MIN. + CHILLING
MAKES: 1 QUART

- 2½ cups seeded sliced banana peppers (about 7 peppers)
- 1 medium green pepper, julienned or 1 medium green tomato, halved and sliced
- 1 jalapeno pepper, seeded and sliced
- 1 small onion, sliced
- ¼ cup canning salt
- 12 to 15 ice cubes
- 2 cups sugar
- 1 cup white vinegar
- 1 tablespoon mustard seed
- ½ teaspoon celery seed

1. In a large bowl, combine the peppers, onion and salt; top with ice. Let stand 2 hours. Rinse and drain well.
2. In a large saucepan, mix remaining ingredients. Bring to a boil; cook and stir just until sugar is dissolved. Pour over pepper mixture; cool. Cover tightly and refrigerate for at least 24 hours. Store an airtight container in the refrigerator up to 3 months.
NOTE *Wear disposable gloves when cutting hot peppers; the oils can burn skin. Avoid touching your face.*

FOOD TRIVIA!
Bread and butter pickles are not too sweet and not too sour. Like Goldilocks' porridge, they are just right. This recipe for bread and butter peppers is also a happy medium.

If your pepper plants are as prolific as mine, this recipe will come in handy. The crunchy mix of sliced peppers and onion makes a zesty picnic side or sandwich topping. —**STARR MILAM** SHELDON, WI

QUICK TOMATO-STRAWBERRY SPREAD

For a creative way to use up tomatoes from you garden, make this spread. The strawberry gelatin gives it a fruity flavor everyone will enjoy.

—MYRA INNES AUBURN, KS

PREP: 5 MIN. • **COOK:** 20 MIN. + STANDING
MAKES: 2⅔ CUPS

- **2 cups chopped peeled ripe tomatoes**
- **1½ cups sugar**
- **1 package (3 ounces) strawberry gelatin**

1. Rinse three 1-cup plastic containers and lids with boiling water. Dry the containers and lids thoroughly. In a large stockpot, bring tomatoes and sugar to a boil over medium-high heat, stirring often. Reduce heat; simmer for 15 minutes. Remove from heat; stir in the gelatin until dissolved. Cool 10 minutes.

2. Fill all containers to within ½ in. of tops. Wipe off top edges of containers; immediately cover with the lids. Cool completely before covering.

3. Refrigerate up to 3 weeks or freeze up to 12 months. Thaw frozen spread in refrigerator before serving.

APPLE & SWEET PEPPER RELISH

PREP: 10 MIN.
COOK: 20 MIN. + CHILLING
MAKES: ABOUT 7 CUPS

- 2 **cups cider vinegar**
- 2 **cups sugar**
- ¾ **teaspoon salt**
- 4 **cups chopped peeled Braeburn or other apples (about 4 medium)**
- 2 **large onions, chopped**
- 1 **medium sweet red pepper, chopped**
- 1 **medium green pepper, chopped**

1. In a nonreactive Dutch oven, combine all the ingredients; bring to a boil. Reduce heat; simmer, uncovered, 10-15 minutes or until the onions are crisp-tender, stirring occasionally. Transfer to a large bowl; cool to room temperature.

2. Refrigerate, covered, at least 6-8 hours before serving. If desired, transfer to covered jars and refrigerate up to 2 weeks.

> Before you turn apples into cobbler or pie, consider making this relish. On burgers, brats or alongside pork, it will be a game changer at your next cookout.
> —**JANETTE SCHULZ** MCDONOUGH, GA

FIG JAM

I have had a love of figs since I had an amazing appetizer that used a combination of figs, blue cheese and prosciutto. Since then, I created this fig jam and have used it as a glaze on our Easter ham, smeared it on a bagel with cream cheese and dolloped it on pizza. It will dress up any dish.

—MONICA KELEHER METHUEN, MA

START TO FINISH: 30 MIN.
MAKES: 2 CUPS

- 2 **cups chopped dried figs**
- 2 **cups water**
- ½ **cup white wine**
- 2 **tablespoons honey**
- 1 **teaspoon grated lemon peel**
- ¼ **teaspoon salt**

1. In a large saucepan, combine figs and water; bring to a boil. Reduce heat; simmer, uncovered, 12-14 minutes or until liquid is almost evaporated, stirring occasionally. Add the wine; cook 6-8 minutes longer or until the liquid is almost evaporated, stirring occasionally.

2. Remove from heat; stir in honey, lemon peel and salt. Cool slightly. Process in a food processor until blended. Transfer to covered jars; refrigerate up to 1 week.

WILD BERRY FREEZER JAM

One year, I decided I wanted to make a wild berry jam but couldn't find a recipe, so I invented my own.

—**BARBARA HOHMANN** PETAWAWA, ON

PREP: 15 MIN. + FREEZING
MAKES: 6 HALF-PINTS

- **1 cup saskatoon berries or blueberries**
- **1 cup raspberries**
- **1 cup strawberries**
- **1 cup blackberries**
- **1 cup blueberries**
- **4 cups sugar**
- **1 pouch (3 ounces) liquid fruit pectin**
- **1 tablespoon lemon juice**

1. Rinse six 1-cup plastic containers and lids with boiling water. Dry the containers and lids thoroughly. In a large bowl, thoroughly crush all of the berries. Stir in sugar; let stand for 10 minutes, stirring occasionally.

2. Combine pectin and lemon juice; add to fruit, stirring constantly until sugar is dissolved, about 3 minutes. (A few sugar crystals may remain.)

3. Immediately fill all containers to within 1/2 in. of tops. Wipe off top edges of containers; immediately cover with lids. Let stand at room temperature for 24 hours.

4. Jam is now ready to use. Refrigerate up to 3 weeks or freeze extra containers up to 12 months. Thaw frozen jam in refrigerator before serving.

NOTE *If saskatoon berries are not available in your area, add an extra cup of one of the other berries.*

ORANGE PINEAPPLE MARMALADE

Here's a sweet and citrusy marmalade that's perfect for spreading on English muffins or biscuits. It also makes a delicious hostess or housewarming gift.

—STEPHANIE HEISE ROCHESTER, NY

PREP: 20 MIN.
COOK: 10 MIN. + STANDING
MAKES: 4 CUPS

- 2 **medium oranges**
- 2 **cans (8 ounces each) crushed pineapple, drained**
- 4 **cups sugar**
- 2 **tablespoons lemon juice**

1. Rinse four 1-cup plastic containers and lids with boiling water. Dry the containers and lids thoroughly.
2. Grate outer peel from oranges and set aside. Peel off and discard white membrane from oranges and section the fruit; discard any seeds. In a food processor, combine orange peel and orange sections; cover and process until orange is in small pieces.
3. In a wide-bottomed microwave-safe 2½-qt. bowl, combine the pineapple, sugar, lemon juice and orange mixture. Microwave, uncovered, on high for 2 to 2½ minutes; stir. Heat for 2 minutes longer (edges will be bubbly); stir. Microwave 1½ to 2 minutes or until mixture is bubbly in center; stir. Heat 2 minutes longer; stir. Cool 10 minutes.
4. Immediately fill all containers to within ½ in. of tops. Wipe off top edges of containers. Cool to room temperature, about 1 hour.
5. Cover and let stand at room temperature for 4 hours. Refrigerate up to 3 weeks or freeze up to 1 year. Thaw the frozen marmalade in refrigerator before serving.
NOTE *This recipe does not use pectin. This recipe was tested in a 1,100-watt microwave.*

PINA COLADA JAM

If you like pina coladas, you'll love this! But here's the kicker: The secret ingredient is fresh zucchini!

—TASTE OF HOME TEST KITCHEN

PREP: 15 MIN.
COOK: 20 MIN. + COOLING
MAKES: 7 CUPS

- 6 **cups sugar**
- 6 **cups shredded peeled zucchini**
- 1 **can (8 ounces) crushed pineapple, undrained**
- ¼ **cup lime juice**
- 2 **packages (3 ounces each) pineapple gelatin**
- 1 **teaspoon rum extract**

1. Rinse seven 1-cup plastic containers and lids with boiling water. Dry the containers and lids thoroughly.
2. In a Dutch oven, bring sugar, zucchini, pineapple and lime juice to a boil. Boil 10 minutes; stir constantly. Remove from heat; stir in gelatin and extract until gelatin is dissolved.
3. Immediately fill all containers to within ½ in. of tops. Wipe off top edges of containers. Cool completely before covering. Refrigerate up to 3 weeks or freeze up to 1 year. Thaw frozen jam in refrigerator before serving.

SUMMER KIMCHI

Ginger enhances these spicy Korean-style pickled veggies. Spoon some on hot dogs for a real treat!

—STEPHEN EXEL DES MOINES, IA

PREP: 30 MIN. + CHILLING
MAKES: 10 CUPS

- 1 **head Chinese or napa cabbage, chopped**
- ⅓ **cup plus 1 tablespoon kosher salt, divided**
- 1 **large cucumber, peeled and thinly sliced**
- 12 **radishes, thinly sliced**
- 4 **green onions, chopped**
- 3 **large garlic cloves, thinly sliced**
- 1 **piece peeled fresh gingerroot (1 inch), sliced**
- 3 **quarts water**
- ¼ **cup rice vinegar**
- 1 **tablespoon Asian red chili paste**

1. Place cabbage in a colander over a plate; sprinkle with ⅓ cup salt and toss. Let stand 30 minutes. Rinse and drain well. In a very large container, combine cabbage, cucumber, radishes, onions, garlic and ginger.

2. In a large bowl, combine the water, vinegar, chili paste and remaining salt; pour over vegetable mixture. Cover and refrigerate for at least 2 days before serving, stirring occasionally. May be transferred to small airtight containers and stored in the refrigerator for up to 3 weeks. Serve with a slotted spoon.

REFRIGERATOR PICKLES

These pickles are so good and easy to prepare, you'll want to keep them on hand all the time. My in-laws send over produce just so I'll make more!

—LOY JONES ANNISTON, AL

PREP: 25 MIN. + CHILLING
MAKES: 6 CUPS

- 3 **cups sliced peeled cucumbers**
- 3 **cups sliced peeled yellow summer squash**
- 2 **cups chopped sweet onions**
- 1½ **cups white vinegar**
- 1 **cup sugar**
- ½ **teaspoon salt**
- ½ **teaspoon celery seed**
- ½ **teaspoon mustard seed**

1. Place cucumbers, squash and onions in a large bowl; set aside. In a small saucepan, combine the remaining ingredients; bring to a boil. Cook and stir just until the sugar is dissolved. Pour over the cucumber mixture; cool.

2. Cover tightly and refrigerate at least 24 hours. Serve with a slotted spoon.

SPICY TOMATO JUICE

You can drink this juice plain or use it in recipes like chili that call for vegetable juice as an ingredient.

—KATHLEEN GILL BUTTE, MT

PREP: 25 MIN. + FREEZING
COOK: 45 MIN. + COOLING
MAKES: ABOUT 5 QUARTS

- **13 pounds ripe tomatoes (about 40 medium)**
- **2 celery ribs, coarsely chopped**
- **3 medium onions, coarsely chopped**
- **1 medium green pepper, coarsely chopped**
- **1½ cups chopped fresh parsley**
- **½ cup sugar**
- **1 tablespoon Worcestershire sauce**
- **4 teaspoons salt**
- **¼ teaspoon hot pepper sauce**
- **¼ teaspoon cayenne pepper**
- **¼ teaspoon pepper**

1. Quarter the tomatoes; place in a 6-qt. Dutch oven. Add celery, onions, green pepper and parsley. Simmer, uncovered, until vegetables are tender, about 45 minutes, stirring occasionally.
2. Meanwhile, rinse five 1-quart plastic containers and lids with boiling water. Dry thoroughly. Cool tomato mixture slightly; put through a sieve or food mill. Return to pan. Add the remaining ingredients; mix well. Bring to a boil. Remove from heat; cool.
3. Fill all containers to within ½ in. of tops. Wipe off top edges of containers; immediately cover with lids. Freeze up to 12 months. Thaw frozen juice in refrigerator before serving.

I love making and enjoying this jam, but I usually end up giving most of it away! It's always well received.
—**LAVONNE VAN HOFF** ROCKWELL CITY, IA

RASPBERRY RHUBARB JAM

PREP: 5 MIN. + COOLING
COOK: 35 MIN. + COOLING
MAKES: 6 CUPS

- **6 cups sliced fresh or frozen rhubarb**
- **4 cups sugar**
- **1 package (6 ounces) raspberry gelatin**
- **1 can (21 ounces) raspberry pie filling**

1. In a large saucepan, combine the rhubarb and sugar; cover and refrigerate overnight.
2. Place saucepan over medium heat; bring to a boil. Reduce heat; simmer, uncovered, 30-35 minutes or until rhubarb is tender. Meanwhile, rinse six 1-cup plastic containers and lids with boiling water. Dry thoroughly.
3. Stir in gelatin and pie filling into rhubarb mixture. Bring to a boil. Remove from heat; cool.
4. Fill all containers to within ½ in. of tops. Wipe off top edges of containers; immediately cover with lids. Refrigerate up to 3 weeks or freeze up to 1 year. Thaw frozen jam in the refrigerator before serving.

ORANGE BLUEBERRY FREEZER JAM

This jam lets me savor the great taste of fresh-picked blueberries no matter the season, but I have to fight my kids for them since they start eating the berries as soon as I pick them.

—MARK MORGAN WATERFORD, WI

PREP: 25 MIN. + STANDING
MAKES: 4 CUPS

- **2½ cups sugar**
- **1 medium orange**
- **1½ cups fresh blueberries, crushed**
- **1 pouch (3 ounces) liquid fruit pectin**

1. Rinse four clean 1-cup plastic containers with lids with boiling water. Dry thoroughly.
2. Preheat oven to 250°. Place sugar in a shallow baking dish; bake 15 minutes. Meanwhile, finely grate 1 tablespoon peel from orange. Peel and chop orange.
3. In a large bowl, combine blueberries, warm sugar, grated peel and chopped orange; let stand 10 minutes, stirring occasionally. Add the pectin; stir constantly for 3 minutes to evenly distribute the pectin.
4. Immediately fill all containers to within ½ in. of tops. Wipe off top edges of containers; immediately cover with lids. Let stand at room temperature 24 hours.
5. Jam is now ready to use. Refrigerate up to 3 weeks or freeze up to 12 months. Thaw frozen jam in the refrigerator before serving.
NOTE *When grating citrus fruits be sure to grate only the outside of the peel—the white pith will make the peel bitter.*

ROASTED BEET JAM

PREP: 1½ HOURS • **COOK:** 1 HOUR
MAKES: 2 HALF-PINTS

2½ **pounds fresh beets**
   (about 10 small)
1 **tablespoon canola oil**
1 **medium lemon**
1 **cinnamon stick (3 inches)**
8 **whole cloves**
1 **cup sugar**
1 **cup packed brown sugar**
⅓ **cup maple syrup**
2 **tablespoons finely chopped crystallized**
   ginger
⅛ **teaspoon salt**

1. Preheat oven to 400°. Peel beets and cut into wedges. Place in a 15x10x1-in. baking pan; drizzle with oil and toss to coat. Roast 50-60 minutes or until tender. Cool slightly.
2. Meanwhile, rinse two 1-cup plastic containers and lids with boiling water. Dry thoroughly. Cut a thin slice from the top and bottom of the lemon; stand lemon upright on a cutting board. With a knife, cut off peel and outer membrane from lemon. Cut in half. Thinly slice half of lemon and remove seeds. (Save remaining half for another use.) Place cinnamon and cloves on a double thickness of cheesecloth. Gather corners of cloth to enclose seasonings; tie securely with string.
3. Place beets in a food processor; pulse until finely chopped. Transfer to a large saucepan. Add sugars, maple syrup, ginger, salt, sliced lemon and spice bag; bring to a boil. Reduce heat; simmer, uncovered, for 1 to 1¼ hours or until thickened. Remove from the heat; discard the spice bag. Cool slightly.
4. Fill containers to within ½ in. of tops. Wipe off top edges of containers; immediately cover with lids. Refrigerate up to 1 week or freeze up to 12 months. Thaw frozen jam in refrigerator before serving.

My spicy jam is a recipe from my Russian grandma, who had no written recipes and who gave jars of the jam as gifts. I re-created the recipe from memory and think of her every time I prepare it.

—SUSAN ASANOVIC WILTON, CT

1. In a large bowl, combine vegetables; sprinkle with salt and cover with cold water. Let stand for 3 hours; rinse and drain.

2. In a large saucepan, bring the remaining ingredients to a boil. Stir in zucchini mixture and return to a boil. Reduce heat; simmer, uncovered, for 5 minutes. Transfer to a large bowl; cool to room temperature. Cover and refrigerate for at least 2 days.

GERMAN-STYLE PICKLED EGGS

I make these eggs and refrigerate them in a glass gallon jar for my husband to sell at his tavern, and the customers can't get enough of them. I found the recipe years ago in an old cookbook.

—MARJORIE HENNIG GREEN VALLEY, AZ

PREP: 20 MIN. + CHILLING
MAKES: 12 SERVINGS

- 2 **cups cider vinegar**
- 1 **cup sugar**
- ½ **cup water**
- 2 **tablespoons prepared mustard**
- 1 **tablespoon salt**
- 1 **tablespoon celery seed**
- 1 **tablespoon mustard seed**
- 6 **whole cloves**
- 2 **medium onions, thinly sliced**
- 12 **hard-cooked eggs, peeled**

1. In a large saucepan, combine the first eight ingredients. Bring to a boil. Reduce heat; cover and simmer for 10 minutes. Cool completely.

2. Place onions and eggs in a large jar; add enough vinegar mixture to completely cover. Cover and refrigerate at least 8 hours or overnight. Use a clean spoon each time you remove eggs for serving. Refrigerate up to 1 week.

ZUCCHINI RELISH

Mom likes to make this crisp and colorful relish when zucchini is in season and Dad's little patch is bursting with veggies.

—NANCY KREISER LEBANON, PA

PREP: 20 MIN. + STANDING
COOK: 15 MIN. + CHILLING
MAKES: 4 CUPS

- 4 **cups diced zucchini**
- 1 **large onion, thinly sliced**
- 2 **celery ribs, sliced**
- 2 **medium carrots, sliced**
- 1 **medium sweet red pepper, sliced**
- 2 **tablespoons salt**
- ¾ **cup sugar**
- ½ **cup water**
- ½ **cup cider vinegar**
- ½ **teaspoon celery seed**
   Dash onion salt
   Dash ground turmeric

KOOL-AID PICKLES

Everyone will love getting into these pickles. They owe their color and sweetly sour taste to a long marinade in a fruity drink mix.

—TASTE OF HOME TEST KITCHEN

PREP: 10 MIN. + CHILLING
MAKES: 3 CUPS

- **1 jar (32 ounces) whole dill pickles, undrained**
- **⅔ cup sugar**
- **1 envelope unsweetened Kool-Aid mix, flavor of your choice**

1. Drain pickles, reserving juice. In a small bowl, combine the reserved juice, sugar and Kool-Aid, stirring until sugar is dissolved. Set aside.

2. Slice pickles; return to jar. Pour juice mixture over pickles. Discard any remaining juice. Cover and refrigerate for 1 week before serving. Store in the refrigerator up to 2 months.

ORANGE JELLY

For a change of pace, try this yummy jelly made from frozen orange juice. I've given it as a gift to friends and family, and many times they kindly return the jars, so I don't run out. Of course, they hope I'll just refill the jars and give them another sample!

—MARY RICE MAYSVILLE, OK

PREP: 5 MIN. • **COOK:** 15 MIN. + STANDING
MAKES: 6 CUPS

- 2⅓ cups water
- 1 can (12 ounces) frozen orange juice concentrate, thawed
- 1 package (1¾ ounces) powdered fruit pectin
- 4½ cups sugar

1. Rinse six 1-cup plastic containers and lids with boiling water. Dry thoroughly. In a Dutch oven or large stockpot, combine water, orange juice concentrate and pectin. Cook and stir until mixture comes to a full rolling boil. Add sugar; return to a full rolling boil. Boil 2 minutes, stirring constantly.

2. Remove from heat; skim off foam if necessary. Immediately fill all the containers to within ½ in. of tops. Wipe off top edges of containers; cool to room temperature, about 1 hour. Cover and let stand overnight or until set. But not longer than 24 hours.

3. Jelly is now ready to use. Refrigerate for up to 3 weeks or freeze up to 1 year. Thaw frozen jelly in the refrigerator before serving.

TUSCAN SUN-DRIED TOMATO JAM

Tomato jam? You bet! My jam has a robust flavor that complements anything it's served with. The taste and texture also make it a yummy substitute for tomato paste.
—**BARB MILLER** OAKDALE, MN

PREP: 15 MIN. • **COOK:** 55 MIN.
MAKES: 1½ CUPS

- **1** jar (7 ounces) oil-packed sun-dried tomatoes
- **½** medium onion, thinly sliced
- **1** garlic clove, minced
- **1** cup water
- **½** cup chicken stock
- **¼** cup red wine vinegar
- **1** tablespoon sugar
- **1** teaspoon dried basil
- **½** teaspoon salt
- **½** teaspoon pepper

1. Drain tomatoes, reserving 1 tablespoon of the oil. Finely chop tomatoes. In a large saucepan, saute tomatoes and onion in reserved oil until onion is tender. Add garlic; cook 1 minute longer.

2. Stir in the water, stock, vinegar, sugar, basil, salt and pepper. Bring to a boil. Reduce heat; cover and simmer for 30 minutes. Uncover; simmer for 15-20 minutes or until liquid has evaporated and the mixture is the consistency of jam. Serve or transfer to an airtight container. Refrigerate up to 1 week.

GREEN TOMATO JAM

As the tomato season draws near and you have a bumper crop of green tomatoes on your vine, reach for this one-of-a-kind jam! Everyone is pleased with its great taste.

—NORMA HENDERSON HAMPTON, NB

PREP: 30 MIN. + COOLING
MAKES: ABOUT 3 CUPS

2½ **cups pureed green tomatoes (about 3 medium)**
2 **cups sugar**
1 **package (3 ounces) raspberry gelatin**

1. In a large saucepan, bring the tomatoes and sugar to a boil. Reduce heat; simmer, uncovered, 20 minutes. Remove from heat; stir in gelatin until dissolved.

2. Skim off any foam. Immediately fill containers to within ½ in. of tops. Wipe off the top edges of containers. Cool completely before covering with lids. Refrigerate up to 3 weeks.

What should you do with your end-of-summer green tomatoes? Gather the last of your garden's green tomatoes before winter's frost damages them. They're delicious when used in the recipe above, but their firm flesh and tart taste also make them ideal for pickling and frying.

FREEZER RASPBERRY SAUCE

This is a great topping for ice cream and since it's thicker than sweetened berries, it's nice over sponge cake or shortcake, too!

—KATIE KOZIOLEK HARTLAND, MN

PREP: 20 MIN. + STANDING
MAKES: 4 PINTS

- 10 **cups fresh raspberries, divided**
- 3 **cups sugar**
- 1 **cup light corn syrup**
- 1 **package (3 ounces) liquid fruit pectin**
- 2 **tablespoons lemon juice**

1. Rinse four 1-pint plastic containers and lids with boiling water. Dry the containers and lids thoroughly.
2. Thoroughly crush 6 cups of the raspberries, 1 cup at a time, to measure exactly 3 cups; transfer to a large bowl. Stir in sugar and corn syrup; let stand 10 minutes, stirring occasionally.
3. In a small bowl, mix liquid pectin and lemon juice. Add to raspberry mixture; stir constantly for 3 minutes to evenly distribute pectin. Stir in remaining whole raspberries.
4. Immediately fill all containers to within 1/2 in. of tops. Wipe off top edges of containers; immediately cover with lids. Let stand at room temperature 24 hours or until partially set.
5. Sauce is now ready to use. Refrigerate up to 3 weeks or freeze up to 12 months. Thaw the frozen sauce in refrigerator before serving.

ORANGE PEAR JAM

I came up with this recipe when a neighbor gave me an armload of pears. It's jam-packed with fruity flavor and is a nice change of pace from strawberry.

—DELORES WARD DECATUR, IN

PREP: 20 MIN.
COOK: 20 MIN. + STANDING
MAKES: ABOUT 7 CUPS

- 7 **cups sugar**
- 5 **cups chopped peeled fresh pears**
- 1 **cup crushed pineapple, drained**
- 2 **tablespoons lemon juice**
- 2 **packages (3 ounces each) orange gelatin**

1. In a Dutch oven, combine sugar, pears, pineapple and lemon juice. Bring to a full rolling boil over high heat, stirring constantly. Reduce heat; simmer 15 minutes, stirring frequently. Remove from heat; stir in the gelatin until dissolved.
2. Pour into jars or containers; cool to room temperature, about 1 hour. Cover and let stand overnight or until set, but no longer than 24 hours. Refrigerate up to 3 weeks.

PEACH RASPBERRY JAM

Back when my children were young, I put up about 100 jars of jams and jellies each summer, including this freezer version. Although I don't make that many now, I stir up a batch to give to neighbors every year.

—DONN WHITE WOOSTER, OH

PREP: 10 MIN.
COOK: 10 MIN. + STANDING
MAKES: ABOUT 5 CUPS

- 1¼ **cups finely chopped peaches**
- 2 **cups fresh raspberries**
- 2 **tablespoons lemon juice**
- 4 **cups sugar**
- ¾ **cup water**
- 1 **package (1¾ ounces) powdered fruit pectin**

1. Rinse five 1-cup plastic containers and lids with boiling water. Dry the containers and lids thoroughly.

2. Place peaches in a large bowl. In a small bowl, mash raspberries; strain to remove seeds if desired. Add raspberries and lemon juice to peaches. Stir in sugar. Let stand 10 minutes. In a small saucepan, bring water and pectin to a full rolling boil. Boil 1 minute, stirring constantly. Add to fruit mixture; stir 2-3 minutes or until sugar is dissolved.

3. Immediately fill all containers to within ½ in. of tops. Wipe off the top edges of containers. Cool to room temperature, about 30 minutes. Cover and let stand overnight or until set, but not longer than 24 hours.

4. Jam is now ready to use. Refrigerate for up to 3 weeks or freeze up to 1 year. Thaw the frozen jam in refrigerator before serving.

CORNCOB JELLY

Making this jelly every year in the summer is a tradition in my family. I love giving this jelly as a homemade gift to friends.

—MARGE HAGY BREWSTER, WA

START TO FINISH: 30 MIN.
MAKES: 5 CUPS

- **12 large corncobs**
- **4 cups water**
- **1 package (1¾ ounces) powdered fruit pectin**
- **4 cups sugar**
  Yellow food coloring

1. Cut corn kernels from cobs and reserve for another recipe. In a stockpot, place corncobs and water; bring to a boil. Cook, uncovered, 10 minutes.

2. Discard the cobs; strain liquid through cheesecloth. Liquid should measure 3 cups. Add additional water if necessary.

3. Return to stockpot and stir in pectin. Bring to a full rolling boil. Add sugar and bring back to a boil. Skim foam and add a few drops of food coloring. Transfer to covered jars; refrigerate up to 2 weeks.

FIRE-AND-ICE PICKLES

PREP: 10 MIN. + CHILLING
MAKES: 3 PINTS

- 2 **jars (32 ounces each) dill pickle slices or spears**
- 4 **cups sugar**
- 1 **tablespoon hot pepper sauce**
- ½ **teaspoon crushed red pepper flakes**
- 3 **garlic cloves, peeled**

Drain and discard juice from pickles. In a large bowl, combine pickles, sugar, pepper sauce and pepper flakes; mix well. Cover and let stand for 2 hours, stirring occasionally. Spoon the pickle mixture into three 1-pint jars; add a garlic clove to each. Cover and refrigerate for 1 week before serving. Store in refrigerator up to 1 month.

These sweet and spicy pickles are great on a sandwich or all by themselves as a snack. The recipe is an easy way to dress up store-bought pickles and make them a special treat! I like to wrap a pretty ribbon around the tops of the jars and give them as gifts.
—MYRA INNES AUBURN, KS

CHUNKY PEACH SPREAD

Here's a fruit spread that captures the best taste of late summer. I like that it's low in sugar and not overly sweet, which lets the fresh peach flavor shine right through.
—**REBECCA BAIRD** SALT LAKE CITY, UT

PREP: 20 MIN.
COOK: 10 MIN. + COOLING
MAKES: ABOUT 3½ CUPS

- 7 **medium peaches (2 to 2½ pounds)**
- 1 **envelope unflavored gelatin**
- ¼ **cup cold water**
- ⅓ **cup sugar**
- 1 **tablespoon lemon juice**

1. Fill a large saucepan two-thirds full with water; bring to a boil. Cut a shallow X on the bottom of each peach. Using tongs, place peaches, a few at a time, in boiling water for 30-60 seconds or just until the skin at the X begins to loosen. Remove peaches and immediately drop into ice water. Pull off skins with tip of a knife; discard skins. Chop peaches.
2. In a small bowl, sprinkle gelatin over cold water; let stand for 1 minute.
3. Meanwhile, in a large saucepan, combine peaches, sugar and lemon juice; bring to a boil. Mash peaches. Reduce heat; simmer, uncovered, for 5 minutes. Add gelatin mixture; cook 1 minute longer, stirring until gelatin is completely dissolved. Cool 10 minutes.
4. Pour into jars. Refrigerate, covered, for up to 3 weeks.

GINGER PEAR FREEZER JAM

PREP: 30 MIN.
COOK: 10 MIN. + STANDING
MAKES: 7 CUPS

- 5½ **cups finely chopped peeled fresh pears (about 10 medium)**
- 1 **package (1¾ ounces) pectin for lower sugar recipes**
- 2 **tablespoons lemon juice**
- 1½ **teaspoons grated lemon peel**
- 1 **teaspoon minced fresh gingerroot**
- 4 **cups sugar**
- 1 **teaspoon vanilla extract**

1. Rinse seven 1-cup plastic containers and lids with boiling water. Dry the containers and lids thoroughly. In a Dutch oven, combine pears, pectin, lemon juice, lemon peel and ginger. Bring to a full rolling boil over high heat, stirring constantly. Stir in sugar. Boil for 1 minute; stir constantly. Stir in vanilla.
2. Remove from heat; skim off foam. Immediately fill all containers to within ½ in. of tops. Wipe off the top edges of containers; immediately cover with lids. Let stand at room temperature for 24 hours.
3. Jam is now ready to use. Refrigerate up to 3 weeks or freeze extra containers up to 12 months. Thaw frozen jam in refrigerator before serving.

At dinner with friends one evening, the lady of the house served us some pears she had preserved with ginger and lemon. The flavor was so heavenly, I decided to use the fresh pears she gave us to try my hand at a ginger and lemon freezer jam.

—**JENI PITTARD** STATHAM, GA

The knobby root known as gingerroot has a peppery taste and spicy aroma. Purchase fresh gingerroot with a smooth skin. If wrinkled and cracked, the root is dry. When stored in a freezer bag, unpeeled gingerroot can be frozen up to 1 year.

EASY APRICOT JAM

Here's the perfect topping for English muffins or toast. It's so simple to make my homemade jam, you'll want to share it with all your friends and family.

—GERI DAVIS PRESCOTT, AZ

PREP: 5 MIN. • **COOK:** 30 MIN. + CHILLING
MAKES: 4 CUPS

- **16 ounces dried apricots**
- **2½ cups orange juice**
- **¾ cup sugar**
- **1 tablespoon lemon juice**
- **½ teaspoon ground cinnamon**
- **¼ teaspoon ground ginger**

1. In a large stockpot, combine apricots, orange juice and sugar; bring to a boil. Reduce heat; cover and simmer for 30 minutes. Stir in lemon juice, cinnamon and ginger. Remove from heat and cool to room temperature.

2. Rinse four 1-cup plastic containers and lids with boiling water. Dry thoroughly. Puree apricot mixture in a food processor or blender until smooth. Spoon into containers, leaving ½-in. headspace. Refrigerate up to 3 weeks or freeze up to 1 year. Thaw frozen jam in refrigerator before serving.

EASY REFRIGERATOR PICKLES

If you don't have nine days to spend on pickling your cukes, or just want a smaller batch, try this incredibly simple recipe.

—CATHERINE SEIBOLD ELMA, NY

PREP: 20 MIN. + CHILLING
MAKES: 6 CUPS

- **6 cups thinly sliced cucumbers**
- **2 cups thinly sliced onions**
- **1½ cups sugar**
- **1½ cups cider vinegar**
- **½ teaspoon salt**
- **½ teaspoon mustard seed**
- **½ teaspoon celery seed**
- **½ teaspoon ground turmeric**
- **½ teaspoon ground cloves**

Place cucumbers and onions in a large bowl; set aside. Combine remaining ingredients in a saucepan; bring to a boil. Cook and stir just until the sugar is dissolved. Pour over cucumber mixture; cool. Cover tightly and refrigerate for at least 24 hours before serving.

PICKLED MUSHROOMS FOR A CROWD

Serve tangy pickled mushrooms alongside a steak, as an appetizer with toothpicks, in a salad or as part of an antipasto platter.

—JOHN LEVEZOW EAGAN, MN

PREP: 15 MIN.
COOK: 15 MIN. + CHILLING
MAKES: ABOUT 7½ DOZEN
(6 CUPS MIXTURE)

- 3 **pounds medium fresh mushrooms**
- 8 **cups water**
- 2 **cups sugar**
- 2 **cups white vinegar**
- 2 **cups dry red wine**
- 3 **tablespoons bitters**
- 1 **teaspoon onion powder**
- 1 **teaspoon garlic salt**
- 1 **teaspoon beef bouillon granules**
- 1 **bay leaf**

1. In a large saucepan, combine the mushrooms and water. Bring to a boil; boil for 1 minute. Drain; return the mushrooms to pan.
2. In a small saucepan, combine the remaining ingredients; bring to a boil, stirring constantly. Pour over mushrooms; cool slightly.
3. Transfer mushroom mixture to glass jars with tight-fitting lids. Cover and refrigerate for at least 2 days. Just before serving, discard bay leaf.

HARVEST CHUTNEY

Seal the best of autumn flavors into a condiment that's delicious any time of year.

—WENDY BALL BATTLE CREEK, MI

PREP: 30 MIN. • **COOK:** 20 MIN.
MAKES: 3½ CUPS

- ⅓ **cup sugar**
- ¼ **cup water**
- 4 **medium apples, peeled and chopped**
- 2 **cups fresh or frozen cranberries**
- 5 **shallots, chopped**
- ⅓ **cup packed brown sugar**
- ¼ **cup cider vinegar**
- ¼ **cup cranberry juice**
- ¼ **cup orange juice**
- 4 **teaspoons grated orange peel**
- ½ **teaspoon salt**
- ½ **teaspoon white pepper**
- ½ **teaspoon ground cinnamon**
- ¼ **teaspoon ground ginger**
- ⅛ **teaspoon ground cloves**
- ½ **cup chopped pecans, toasted**

1. In a large saucepan, bring sugar and water to a boil over medium heat. Stir in apples, cranberries, shallots, brown sugar, vinegar, cranberry juice, orange juice, peel and seasonings.
2. Return to a boil. Reduce heat; simmer, uncovered, 15-20 minutes or until desired thickness, stirring occasionally. Stir in pecans. Cool. Spoon into jars. Cover and store in the refrigerator up to 3 weeks.

STRAWBERRY JAM IN A JIFFY

Most people put jam on homemade biscuits, but not me. I love slathering a little butter and this amazing strawberry jam on a piping hot piece of corn bread just out of the oven; it's incredible.

—MICHELLE ROBERTS GREENDALE, WI

PREP: 20 MIN. + STANDING
COOK: 10 MIN. + STANDING
MAKES: 4½ CUPS

- 4 **cups fresh strawberries, hulled**
- 4 **cups sugar**
- ¾ **cup water**
- 1 **package (1¾ ounces) powdered fruit pectin**

1. Rinse five 1-cup freezer-safe containers and lids with boiling water. Dry thoroughly. Thoroughly crush strawberries, 1 cup at a time, to measure exactly 2 cups; transfer to a large bowl. Stir in sugar; let stand for 10 minutes, stirring occasionally.

2. In a small saucepan, mix water and pectin; bring to a boil over high heat, stirring constantly. Boil 1 minute longer. Add to strawberry mixture, stirring until sugar is dissolved, about 3 minutes. (A few sugar crystals may remain.)

3. Immediately fill all containers to within ½ in. of tops. Wipe off top edges of containers; immediately cover with lids. Let stand at room temperature 24 hours.

4. Jam is now ready to use. Refrigerate up to 3 weeks or freeze extra containers up to 1 year. Thaw frozen jam in refrigerator before serving.

APRICOT PINEAPPLE JAM

Dried apricots, crushed pineapple and grapefruit juice create a memorable jam. The juice is what makes the jam taste so good.

—CAROL RADIL NEW BRITAIN, CT

PREP: 10 MIN.
COOK: 1 HOUR 20 MIN. + STANDING
MAKES: 5 CUPS

- 12 **ounces dried apricots**
- 1 **cup water**
- 1 **can (20 ounces) crushed pineapple, undrained**
- ½ **cup grapefruit juice**
- 3 **cups sugar**

1. In a large saucepan, bring apricots and water to a boil. Reduce heat; cover and simmer 15 minutes or until apricots are very tender. Mash. Add pineapple, grapefruit juice and sugar. Simmer, uncovered, 1 hour or until thick and translucent, stirring frequently.

2. Rinse five 1-cup plastic containers and lids with boiling water. Dry thoroughly. Pour jam into containers; cool to room temperature, about 1 hour. Cover and let stand overnight or until set, but no longer than 24 hours.

3. Jam is now ready to use. Refrigerate up to 3 weeks or freeze up to 1 year. Thaw frozen jam in the refrigerator before serving.

NOTE *This recipe does not use pectin.*

ZUCCHINI PEACH JELLY

I like to use this jelly as a condiment. It's always a conversation piece...everyone wonders about the green ingredient! This beautiful jelly is so easy to make and I use it as a gift-giving item during the holidays.

—RUTH GLICK DALTON, OH

PREP: 5 MIN. • **COOK:** 15 MIN. + COOLING
MAKES: 7½ PINTS

- **6 cups shredded peeled zucchini (about 4 medium)**
- **6 cups sugar**
- **2 tablespoons lemon juice**
- **1 can (8 ounces) crushed pineapple with juice**
- **2 packages (3 ounces each) peach or orange gelatin**

1. In a large saucepan or Dutch oven, combine zucchini, sugar, lemon juice and pineapple with juice; bring to a boil. Cook, stirring often, at a full boil 10 minutes.

2. Remove from heat; stir in gelatin. Spoon into clean jelly jars. Cover and cool. Store in the refrigerator for up to 3 weeks.

CHRISTMAS PICKLES

My pickle recipe was adapted from one a dear family friend shared. These morsels are delicious any time of year, but the green, red and white hues of this mixture make them ideal for Christmas gift giving.

—PATRICIA MARTIN SHELBYVILLE, TN

PREP: 10 MIN. • **COOK:** 25 MIN. + CHILLING
MAKES: 6½ QUARTS

- 1 **gallon whole dill pickles**
- 1¼ **cups sugar**
- 1 **cup white vinegar**
- 1 **tablespoon mustard seed**
- 1 **tablespoon whole cloves**
- 3 **to 4 jalapeno peppers, chopped**
- 4 **to 5 garlic cloves, minced**
- 4 **to 5 whole cinnamon sticks**
- 1 **pound whole candied cherries**
- 3 **jars (15 ounces each) pearl onions, drained**
- 1 **teaspoon olive oil**

1. Drain pickles; reserving juice; set juice aside. Cut pickles into ½-in. slices; set aside. In a large stockpot, combine sugar, vinegar, mustard seed, cloves, peppers, garlic, cinnamon sticks and pickle juice.
2. Cook over medium heat 10 minutes or until sugar is dissolved, stirring occasionally. Bring to a boil. Reduce heat; simmer, uncovered, 10 minutes. Remove from heat; cool slightly. Discard cinnamon sticks.
3. In a large bowl, combine cherries, onions and pickle slices. Pour liquid over pickle mixture. Stir in oil.
4. Cover and refrigerate for 48 hours, stirring occasionally. Divide mixture among jars. Cover and store in the refrigerator up to 1 month.
NOTE *Wear disposable gloves when cutting hot peppers; the oils can burn skin. Avoid touching your face.*

FREEZER SALSA JAM

This is a great addition to any Mexican dish. I made it from combining a friend's recipe and a recipe from a canning cookbook.

—ELLEN KATZKE DELAVAN, MN

PREP: 30 MIN.
COOK: 10 MIN. + STANDING
MAKES: 4½ CUPS

- 2 **cups finely chopped plum tomatoes (6 to 7)**
- ½ **cup finely chopped onion**
- 1 **can (8 ounces) tomato sauce**
- ¼ **cup chopped fresh cilantro**
- ¼ **cup finely chopped fresh or canned jalapeno peppers**
- 2 **tablespoons lime juice**
- 1 **teaspoon grated lime peel**
- ¼ **teaspoon hot pepper sauce**
- 1½ **cups sugar**
- 1 **package (1¾ ounces) pectin for lower sugar recipes**
- ¼ **cup water**

1. Rinse five 1-cup plastic containers and lids with boiling water. Dry thoroughly. In a large bowl, combine tomatoes, onion, tomato sauce, cilantro, peppers, lime juice, peel and hot pepper sauce; set aside.

2. In a large saucepan, combine sugar and pectin; stir in water. Bring to a boil; boil and stir 1 minute. Remove from heat. Stir in tomato mixture; continue to stir until well combined.

3. Immediately fill containers to within ½ in. of tops. Wipe off top edges of containers. Cool to room temperature, about 1 hour. Cover and let stand at room temperature 24 hours.

4. Jam is now ready to use. Refrigerate up to 3 weeks or freeze up to 1 year. Thaw the frozen jam in refrigerator before serving.

NOTE *Wear disposable gloves when cutting hot peppers; the oils can burn skin. Avoid touching your face.*

REFRIGERATOR GARDEN PICKLES

PREP: 20 MIN.
COOK: 15 MIN. + CHILLING
MAKES: 7 PINTS

- 6 **cups sugar**
- 6 **cups white vinegar**
- ¼ **cup celery seed**
- ¼ **cup mustard seed**
- 2 **tablespoons canning salt**
- 10 **medium carrots, halved and quartered**
- 3 **medium cucumbers, sliced**
- 3 **medium sweet red peppers, cut into 1-inch pieces**
- 2 **large onions, halved and sliced**
- 1 **bunch green onions, cut into 2-inch pieces**

1. In a Dutch oven, combine the first five ingredients; bring to a boil, stirring to dissolve sugar. Meanwhile, place the remaining ingredients in a large bowl.

2. Pour hot liquid over vegetables; cool. Transfer to jars, if desired; cover tightly. Refrigerate 6-8 hours before serving. Store in the refrigerator up to 1 month.

No need to can here! You can still get crisp-tender, tangy pickles—just keep them in the fridge and eat them within a month. —**LINDA CHAIPMAN** MERIDEN, IA

EASY HOMEMADE DILL PICKLES

In July, cucumbers are at their peak. Take advantage of garden extras by whipping up a few jars of pickles. My husband grows cucumbers, garlic and dill and eagerly waits for me to make these. The recipe comes from my grandmother.

—ANGELA LIENHARD BLOSSBURG, PA

PREP: 45 MIN. + CHILLING
MAKES: 4½ QUARTS

- 14 **pickling cucumbers**
- 40 **fresh dill sprigs**
- 4 **garlic cloves, sliced**
- 2 **quarts water**
- 1 **cup cider vinegar**
- ½ **cup sugar**
- ⅓ **cup salt**
- 1 **teaspoon mixed pickling spices**

1. Cut each cucumber lengthwise into six spears. In a large bowl, combine cucumbers, dill and garlic; set aside.

2. In a Dutch oven, combine remaining ingredients. Bring to a boil; cook and stir just until sugar is dissolved. Pour over cucumber mixture; cool.

3. Transfer to jars if desired and cover tightly. Refrigerate for at least 24 hours. Store in the refrigerator up to 2 weeks.

STRAWBERRY-KIWI JAM

My family always gives jams and jellies as gifts and everyone appreciates the thought. Strawberries and kiwi make an absolutely wonderful combination.

—**KATHY KITTELL** LENEXA, KS

PREP: 20 MIN.
COOK: 15 MIN. + STANDING
MAKES: 5¾ CUPS

- **6 cups fresh strawberries**
- **3 medium kiwifruit, peeled and finely chopped**
- **1 tablespoon lemon juice**
- **1 tablespoon chopped crystallized ginger**
- **1 package (1¾ ounces) powdered fruit pectin**
- **5 cups sugar**

1. Rinse six 1-cup plastic containers and lids with boiling water. Dry thoroughly. In a large bowl, mash the berries; transfer to a Dutch oven. Add kiwi, lemon juice and ginger. Stir in pectin. Bring to a full rolling boil over high heat, stirring constantly.

2. Stir in sugar; return to a full rolling boil. Boil 1 minute, stirring constantly.

3. Remove from heat; skim off foam. Immediately fill all containers to within ½ in. of tops. Wipe off the top edges of containers and cool to room temperature, about 1 hour. Cover and let stand at room temperature 24 hours.

4. Jam is now ready to use. Refrigerate up to 3 weeks or freeze extra containers up to 12 months. Thaw frozen jam in refrigerator before serving.

> When I first started making these crunchy pickles, I wasn't sure if freezing cucumbers would actually work. To my surprise, they came out perfectly. Now I share them with friends and neighbors.
>
> **—CONNIE GOENSE**
> PEMBROKE PINES, FL

FREEZER CUCUMBER PICKLES

PREP: 20 MIN. + FREEZING
MAKES: 10 PINTS

- 4 **pounds pickling cucumbers, sliced**
- 8 **cups thinly sliced onions (about 8 medium)**
- ¼ **cup salt**
- ¾ **cup water**
- 4 **cups sugar**
- 2 **cups cider vinegar**

1. Rinse ten 2-cup plastic containers and lids with boiling water. Dry thoroughly. Divide cucumbers, onions, salt and water between two large bowls. Let stand at room temperature 2 hours. Do not drain.

2. Add 2 cups sugar and 1 cup vinegar to each bowl; stir until sugar is dissolved. Transfer to prepared containers, leaving 1-in. headspace for expansion; freeze up to 6 weeks.

3. Thaw pickles in refrigerator for 8 hours before using. Serve within 2 weeks after thawing.

What is a pickling cucumber?

Pickling cucumbers are smaller than the common salad cucumber. They also have fewer seeds and a thinner, bumpier skin, which allows the vinegar or brine to better flavor the flesh. Kirby is a popular pickling cucumber variety.

PRETTY PEACH JAM

This has been a favorite jam in my family for as long as I can remember. It's a delicious medley of fruits, including peaches, cherries, pineapple and orange.

—THERESA BECKMAN INWOOD, IA

PREP: 20 MIN.
COOK: 20 MIN. + STANDING
MAKES: 13 CUPS

- **8 medium peaches, peeled and cut into wedges**
- **1 small unpeeled navel orange, cut into wedges**
- **2 cans (8 ounces each) crushed pineapple, undrained**
- **12 maraschino cherries**
- **3 tablespoons maraschino cherry juice**
- **2 packages (1¾ ounces each) powdered fruit pectin**
- **10 cups sugar**

1. Rinse thirteen 1-cup plastic containers and lids with boiling water. Dry thoroughly.

2. In a blender or food processor, cover and process fruits and juice in batches until smooth. Transfer to a large stockpot; stir in pectin and bring to a rolling boil over high heat, stirring frequently. Add the sugar and return to a rolling boil. Boil for 2 minutes, stirring constantly.

3. Remove from heat. Immediately fill all containers to within ½ in. of tops. Wipe off top edges of containers. Immediately cover with lids. Let stand at room temperature 24 hours.

4. Jam is now ready to use. Refrigerate up to 3 weeks or freeze up to 1 year. Thaw frozen jam in refrigerator before serving.

Savory
Sauces &
Condiments

ENCHILADA SAUCE

Here's a chunky, mild sauce that's a great way to use up abundant veggies from the garden. It tastes great on Mexican dishes and scrambled eggs.

—REBECCA SCHWEGMAN ST. CROIX FALLS, WI

PREP: 20 MIN. • **COOK:** 1 HOUR • **MAKES:** 6½ CUPS

- 10 **plum tomatoes**
- 3 **cups water**
- 2 **medium onions, chopped**
- 2 **medium carrots, shredded**
- 1 **medium zucchini, shredded**
- 1 **large sweet red pepper, chopped**
- 1 **cup minced fresh cilantro**
- 2 **jalapeno peppers, seeded and chopped**
- 7 **garlic cloves, minced**
- 2 **tablespoons chili powder**
- 1 **tablespoon salt**
- 1 **tablespoon paprika**
- 1 **teaspoon dried oregano**
- ½ **teaspoon dried thyme**

1. Fill a large saucepan two-thirds with water; bring to a boil. Cut a shallow X on the bottom of each tomato. Using tongs, place tomatoes, a few at a time, in boiling water for 30-60 seconds or just until skin at the X begins to loosen. Remove tomatoes and immediately drop into ice water. Pull off skins with tip of a knife; discard skins.

2. In a Dutch oven, combine the remaining ingredients. Add tomatoes and bring to a boil. Reduce heat; simmer, uncovered, 1-2 hours or until mixture reaches desired consistency.

3. Cool slightly. Process in batches in a blender until smooth. If desired, return all to pan and heat through. Transfer to an airtight container; refrigerate up to 3 days or freeze up to 4 months.

NOTE *Wear disposable gloves when cutting hot peppers; the oils can burn skin. Avoid touching your face.*

1 minute longer. Add the water, peanut butter, sugar and chili powder. Bring to a boil. Cook and stir 2-3 minutes or until slightly thickened.

2. Remove from heat; stir in the lemon juice, soy sauce and salt.

END-OF-SUMMER RELISH

PREP: 45 MIN.
COOK: 1 HOUR + CHILLING
MAKES: 12 CUPS

- 4 **each medium green, sweet red and yellow peppers, cut into 1-inch pieces**
- 4 **medium onions, quartered**
- 4 **medium carrots, cut into 2-inch pieces**
- 2 **medium cucumbers, peeled and cut into 2-inch pieces**
- 1 **small head cabbage, cut into wedges**
- 2¾ **cups white vinegar**
- 1 **cup sugar**
- ¾ **cup water**
- 3 **tablespoons salt**
- 1 **tablespoon mustard seed**
- 1 **tablespoon celery seed**
  Cooked sausage or meat of your choice

1. In a food processor, cover and process the vegetables in batches until finely chopped. Drain the vegetables and discard liquid.

2. In a stockpot, bring vinegar, sugar, water, salt, mustard seed and celery seed to a boil. Add the vegetables; return to a boil. Reduce heat; simmer, uncovered, 1 hour or until thickened. Store in airtight containers in the refrigerator up to 1 week. Serve with sausage or meat.

PEANUT BUTTER DIPPING SAUCE

Use this versatile peanut sauce, with its zippy touch of chili powder, to toss with noodles or marinate meat. Of course, it's a terrific dip for chicken wings, too!

—CHRISTINE OMAR HARWICH PORT, MA

START TO FINISH: 25 MIN.
MAKES: 1⅓ CUPS

- 1 **medium onion, chopped**
- 2 **tablespoons canola oil**
- 2 **garlic cloves, minced**
- ½ **cup water**
- ¼ **cup creamy peanut butter**
- 1 **tablespoon sugar**
- 1 **tablespoon chili powder**
- 2 **tablespoons lemon juice**
- 2 **tablespoons soy sauce**
- ¼ **teaspoon salt**

1. In a small saucepan, saute onion in oil until tender. Add garlic; cook

My family loves this relish and wants it on the table for every meal. My vegetable garden can barely keep up with the demand. —**VIVIAN CONNER** SEBRING, FL

CRANBERRY CHUTNEY

You can serve this chunky chutney over
cream cheese or Brie with crackers, or as
a condiment with roast pork or poultry.
Either way, its slightly tart flavor and deep
red hue lend a festive flair to the table.

—KARYN GORDON ROCKLEDGE, FL

PREP: 40 MIN. + CHILLING
MAKES: 3 CUPS

- **4 cups (1 pound) fresh or frozen cranberries**
- **1 cup sugar**
- **1 cup water**
- **½ cup packed brown sugar**
- **2 teaspoons ground cinnamon**
- **1½ teaspoons ground ginger**
- **½ teaspoon ground cloves**
- **¼ teaspoon ground allspice**
- **1 cup chopped tart apple**
- **½ cup golden raisins**
- **½ cup diced celery**

In a large saucepan, combine the first
eight ingredients. Cook over medium
heat until berries pop, about 15 minutes.
Add the apple, raisins and celery.
Simmer, uncovered, until thickened,
about 15 minutes. Transfer to a small
bowl; refrigerate until chilled.

COFFEE BARBECUE SAUCE

PREP: 15 MIN. • **COOK:** 50 MIN.
MAKES: 4½ CUPS

- 1 **medium onion, finely chopped**
- 2 **tablespoons olive oil**
- 8 **garlic cloves, minced**
- 2 **cups ketchup**
- 1 **cup cider vinegar**
- 1 **cup honey**
- ½ **cup reduced-sodium soy sauce**
- ½ **cup strong brewed coffee**
- 2 **teaspoons instant coffee granules**
- ¼ **teaspoon salt**
- ¼ **teaspoon pepper**

In a large saucepan, saute onion in oil until tender. Add garlic; cook 2 minutes longer. Stir in remaining ingredients and bring to a boil. Reduce heat; simmer, uncovered, 35-45 minutes or until desired consistency, stirring occasionally.

> Brewed coffee and instant coffee granules add rich color and depth to this sweet-and-sour sauce. It's wonderful spooned over grilled chicken or pork chops.
> —**JULIA BUSHREE** COMMERCE CITY, CO

STICKY NOTES

—————————————————
—————————————————
—————————————————
—————————————————
—————————————————
—————————————————
—————————————————
—————————————————
—————————————————
—————————————————
—————————————————
—————————————————
—————————————————
—————————————————
—————————————————
—————————————————
—————————————————
—————————————————
—————————————————
—————————————————
—————————————————
—————————————————
—————————————————
—————————————————
—————————————————
—————————————————
—————————————————
—————————————————
—————————————————
—————————————————
—————————————————
—————————————————
—————————————————
—————————————————
—————————————————
—————————————————
—————————————————
—————————————————
—————————————————
—————————————————
—————————————————

CHIPOTLE SAUCE

I grow a huge garden every year to help feed my family of seven. My sister shared this recipe with me as a way to use up my bounty of tomatoes. You can also puree the mixture to create a barbecue sauce for meats.
—**JEAN KENNEDY** WALTON, OR

PREP: 1 HOUR • **PROCESS:** 15 MIN.
MAKES: 6 HALF-PINTS

- 4 **pounds plum tomatoes (about 12 medium)**
- 1 **cup packed brown sugar**
- ¾ **cup cider vinegar**
- ¼ **cup minced chipotle peppers in adobo sauce**
- 2 **teaspoons salt**

1. In a large saucepan, bring 8 cups water to a boil. Add tomatoes, a few at a time; boil 30 seconds. Drain and immediately place tomatoes in ice water. Drain and pat dry; peel.

2. In a food processor, cover and process tomatoes in batches until finely chopped. Transfer to a Dutch oven. Add brown sugar, vinegar, chipotle peppers and salt. Bring to a boil. Reduce heat; simmer, uncovered, 20-25 minutes or until most of the liquid is evaporated, stirring constantly.

3. Remove from heat. Ladle hot mixture into six hot half-pint jars, leaving ½-in. headspace. Remove the air bubbles and adjust headspace, if necessary, by adding hot mixture. Wipe the rims. Center lids on jars; screw on bands until fingertip tight.

4. Place jars into canner with simmering water, ensuring that they are completely covered with water. Bring to a boil; process for 15 minutes. Remove jars and cool.

NOTE *The processing time listed is for altitudes of 1,000 feet or less. For altitudes up to 3,000 feet, add 5 minutes; 6,000 feet, add 10 minutes; 8,000 feet, add 15 minutes; 10,000 feet, add 20 minutes.*

GARLIC LEMON BUTTER

This tangy flavored butter offers a nice change from plain butter and gives a refreshing new taste to an ear of corn.

—MARGIE WAMPLER BUTLER, PA

START TO FINISH: 10 MIN.
MAKES: ½ CUP

- ½ **cup butter, softened**
- 2 **to 3 teaspoons grated lemon peel**
- 1 **garlic clove, minced**
- 1 **teaspoon minced fresh parsley**
- ¼ **teaspoon salt, optional**
  Pepper to taste

In a small bowl, beat the butter, lemon peel, garlic, parsley, if desired, salt and pepper until blended. Refrigerate up to 1 week or freeze up to 3 months.

SOUTH LIBERTY HALL RELISH

My grandparents originated this recipe that's been treasured in our family for four generations. It's named after a dance hall they ran in rural Iowa.

—MELINDA WINCHELL LAS VEGAS, NV

PREP: 10 MIN. + CHILLING
MAKES: 2 CUPS

- 1 jar (16 ounces) whole dill pickles, drained
- ¼ cup chopped onion
- 2 to 3 tablespoons sugar
- ½ cup yellow mustard

Place the pickles and onion in a food processor; cover and process until finely chopped. Transfer to a bowl; stir in sugar and mustard. Store in an airtight container in the refrigerator up to 1 week.

RASPBERRY BARBECUE SAUCE

Raspberries replace the traditional tomatoes in this unique barbecue sauce. Red pepper flakes add a little kick to the thick ruby-red sauce. This sauce is great over chicken breasts or pork tenderloin. Brush on the sauce near the end of the grilling time.

—GARNET PIRRE HELENA, MT

PREP: 40 MIN. + COOLING
MAKES: 4 SERVINGS

- 3 **garlic cloves, peeled**
- ¼ **teaspoon olive oil**
- 1¼ **cups unsweetened raspberries**
- 3 **tablespoons brown sugar**
- 1 **tablespoon balsamic vinegar**
- 1 **tablespoon light corn syrup**
- 1 **teaspoon molasses**
- ½ **teaspoon lemon juice**
- ¼ to ½ **teaspoon crushed red pepper flakes**
- ⅛ **teaspoon salt**
- ⅛ **teaspoon pepper**
  Dash onion powder

1. Preheat oven to 425°. Place garlic on a double thickness of heavy-duty foil; drizzle with oil. Wrap foil around garlic. Bake 15-20 minutes. Cool 10-15 minutes.

2. Place softened garlic in a small saucepan. Add remaining ingredients. Cook over medium-low heat 15-20 minutes until sauce is thickened and bubbly. Remove from heat; cool slightly.

3. Transfer to a food processor; cover and process until smooth. Strain seeds. Store in an airtight container in the refrigerator.

SPICY OLIVE RELISH

I was looking for a zippy relish to jazz up plain hot dogs. Not wishing to make a run to the store, I rummaged through my refrigerator and found these items and thought they would be good together—and I was right! This condiment also goes well on toasted bagel bites.

—JAMES MACGILLIVRAY SAN MARCOS, CA

START TO FINISH: 10 MIN.
MAKES: 2 CUPS

- 1 **jar (16 ounces) pickled hot cherry peppers, drained**
- 1 **jar (7 ounces) pimiento-stuffed olives, drained**
- 1 **small onion, quartered**
- 1 **tablespoon yellow mustard**

Place peppers, olives and onion in a food processor; cover and process until finely chopped. Transfer to a bowl; stir in mustard.

GINGERED PEACH CHUTNEY

As far as I'm concerned, this recipe features the best fruit of the summer: pears. I love to add this chutney to pork roast or chops.
—MARLENE WICZEK LITTLE FALLS, MN

PREP: 20 MIN. • **COOK:** 50 MIN.
MAKES: 3½ CUPS

- 4 **cups chopped peeled fresh peaches**
- 1½ **cups cider vinegar**
- 1 **cup plus 2 tablespoons packed brown sugar**
- 1 **small onion, finely chopped**
- ½ **cup raisins**
- ⅓ **cup chopped crystallized ginger**
- 1 **tablespoon mustard seed**
- 1 **tablespoon chili powder**
- 1 **teaspoon salt**
- 1 **small garlic clove, minced**

1. In a Dutch oven, combine all the ingredients. Bring to a boil over medium heat. Reduce heat; simmer, uncovered, 45-50 minutes or until thickened and reduced to about 3½ cups, stirring occasionally.
2. Serve warm or at room temperature. Refrigerate leftovers.

RHUBARB KETCHUP

PREP: 5 MIN. • **COOK:** 1 HOUR + CHILLING
MAKES: 6-7 CUPS

- 4 **cups diced fresh or frozen rhubarb**
- 3 **medium onions, chopped**
- 1 **can (28 ounces) diced tomatoes, undrained**
- 1 **cup sugar**
- 1 **cup packed brown sugar**
- 1 **cup white vinegar**
- 2 **teaspoons salt**
- 1 **teaspoon ground cinnamon**
- 1 **tablespoon pickling spice**

1. In a large saucepan, combine the first eight ingredients. Place pickling spice on a double thickness of cheesecloth. Gather corners of cloth to enclose seasoning; tie securely with string. Add to saucepan. Cook 1 hour or until thickened.
2. Discard the spice bag. Cool the ketchup. Store in airtight containers in the refrigerator.

FOOD TRIVIA!
Rhubarb is so popular in Minnesota that there are festivals in both Lanesboro and Duluth. These perennials are easiest to grow in northern states where the ground freezes in winter. However, even those without green thumbs can still get their hands dirty at local pick-your-own rhubarb farms.

I received this recipe from a friend about 15 years ago. It's a nice surprise for ketchup lovers, and so easy to prepare. The spicy flavor makes this one of the tastiest ketchups I've ever had! —**FAITH McLILLIAN** RAWDON, QC

ZUCCHINI SALSA VERDE

My family and friends think this is the best green salsa ever; it's bright and sweet with just the right hint of spice.

—DONNA KELLY PROVO, UT

PREP: 25 MIN. • **GRILL:** 20 MIN.
MAKES: 3 CUPS

- 1 large sweet onion, cut into wedges
- 2 poblano peppers, cut into 1-inch pieces
- 2 medium zucchini, cut into 1-inch pieces
- 4 tomatillos, husks removed and quartered
- 3 jalapeno peppers, halved and seeded
- 2 tablespoons canola oil
- 2 tablespoons lime juice
- 1 tablespoon Louisiana-style hot sauce
- 1½ teaspoons grated lime peel
- ¼ teaspoon salt
- 2 teaspoons honey, optional

1. In a large bowl, combine the first six ingredients. Transfer to a grill wok or basket. Grill vegetables, covered, over medium heat 18-22 minutes or until slightly charred and tender, stirring occasionally.

2. Cool slightly. Finely chop and transfer to a small bowl. Stir in the lime juice, hot sauce, lime peel, salt and if desired, honey.

NOTE *Wear disposable gloves when cutting hot peppers; the oils can burn skin. Avoid touching your face.*

PICKLED PUMPKIN

You can enjoy a taste of autumn for weeks! This turns fresh pumpkin into a tasty topping for pork chops or poultry.

—MYRA INNES AUBURN, KS

PREP: 15 MIN. • **COOK:** 1¼ HOURS
MAKES: 2 CUPS

- **1 cup water**
- **½ cup sugar**
- **1¾ cups cubed peeled pie pumpkin**
- **¼ cup cider vinegar**
- **½ teaspoon whole cloves**

In a large saucepan, bring water and sugar to a boil; cook and stir 5 minutes. Add the pumpkin, vinegar and cloves. Reduce heat; simmer, uncovered, for 1¼ hour s or until pumpkin is tender. Discard cloves. Store in an airtight container in refrigerator up to 3 weeks.

CLASSIC PESTO

Here's a versatile pesto that boasts a perfect basil flavor. Pair it with pasta and you've got a classic Italian dinner.

—IOLA EGLE BELLA VISTA, AR

START TO FINISH: 10 MIN.
MAKES: 1 CUP

- **4 cups loosely packed basil leaves**
- **½ cup grated Parmesan cheese**
- **2 garlic cloves, halved**
- **¼ teaspoon salt**
- **½ cup pine nuts, toasted**
- **½ cup olive oil**

Place the basil, cheese, garlic and salt in a food processor; cover and pulse until chopped. Add nuts; cover and process until blended. While processing, gradually add oil in a steady stream. Store in an airtight container in the freezer up to 1 year.

CRANBERRY BBQ SAUCE

Packed alongside cheese and crackers, this homemade barbecue sauce is a delightful savory gift option.

—DARLA ANDREWS LEWISVILLE, TX

START TO FINISH: 15 MIN.
MAKES: 2⅔ CUPS

- **1 can (14 ounces) whole-berry cranberry sauce**
- **1½ cups barbecue sauce**
- **1 teaspoon ground cinnamon**
- **1 teaspoon chili powder**
- **1 teaspoon ground cumin**
- **1 teaspoon pepper**
- **½ teaspoon salt**
  Gouda cheese and assorted crackers

In a small saucepan, mix the first seven ingredients; heat through. Store in an airtight container in the refrigerator up to 1 month. To serve, reheat sauce and serve with cheese and crackers.

My mother passed her ketchup recipe down to me. It may sound like a strange combination of flavors, but once you try it, you won't want to go back to regular ketchup. **—JEROME WIESE** BEMIDJI, MN

CRANBERRY KETCHUP

PREP: 20 MIN. • **COOK:** 1 HOUR + COOLING
MAKES: 1½ CUPS

- 1 **package (12 ounces) fresh or frozen cranberries**
- 1 **large red onion, chopped**
- 2 **cups water**
- ¾ **cup sugar**
- ½ **cup cider vinegar**
- 1½ **teaspoons salt**
- 1 **cinnamon stick (3 inches)**
- 4 **whole allspice**
- ½ **teaspoon mustard seed**
- ½ **teaspoon whole peppercorns**

1. In a large saucepan, combine the cranberries, onion and water. Cook over medium heat until the berries pop, about 15 minutes. Cool slightly. Transfer to a food processor; cover and process until smooth. Return to the pan and bring to a boil. Reduce heat to medium-low. Cook, uncovered, 20 minutes or until mixture is reduced to 2 cups, stirring frequently.

2. Stir in sugar, vinegar and salt. Place cinnamon, allspice, mustard seed and peppercorns on a double thickness of cheesecloth; bring up corners of cloth and tie with string to form a bag. Add to cranberry mixture. Cook and stir 25-30 minutes or until thickened.

3. Discard spice bag. Cool ketchup. Store in an airtight container in the refrigerator up to 3 weeks.

VIDALIA ONION RELISH

Burgers and brats get the star treatment with this sweet onion topping. Bourbon adds a lovely caramel note, and the crushed pepper flakes turn up the heat.
—**JANET ROTH** TEMPE, AZ

PREP: 1 HOUR • **COOK:** 15 MIN.
MAKES: 3 CUPS

- 4 **large sweet onions, chopped**
- 2 **tablespoons canola oil**
- 3 **garlic cloves, minced**
- ⅓ **cup bourbon**
- 4 **plum tomatoes, peeled, seeded and chopped**
- ½ **cup golden raisins**
- ¼ **cup sugar**
- ¼ **cup packed dark brown sugar**
- ¼ **cup cider vinegar**
- 1 **teaspoon mustard seed**
- ½ **teaspoon salt**
- ½ **teaspoon ground turmeric**
- ½ **teaspoon ground mustard**
- ½ **teaspoon crushed red pepper flakes**
- ¼ **teaspoon pepper**

1. In a large saucepan, cook onions in oil over medium heat 40-45 minutes or until onions are golden brown, stirring occasionally. Add garlic; cook 1 minute longer. Remove from heat. Add the bourbon, stirring to loosen browned bits from pan.
2. Stir in remaining ingredients; bring to a boil. Reduce heat; simmer, uncovered, 15-20 minutes or until thickened. Store in airtight containers in the refrigerator up to 1 week. Serve with sausage or meat.

PICKLED MUSHROOMS WITH GARLIC

I'm always asked to bring these tempting tidbits to holiday gatherings. Easy to make ahead and transport, they add a festive touch to a relish tray.
—**JOYCE ANDERSON** CHICO, CA

PREP: 10 MIN. + MARINATING
MAKES: 4½ CUPS

- ⅔ **cup white wine vinegar**
- ½ **cup canola oil**
- 2 **tablespoons water**
- 1 **teaspoon salt**
  Dash pepper
  Dash hot pepper sauce
- 1 **pound small whole fresh mushrooms**
- 1 **medium onion, thinly sliced**
- 2 **to 4 garlic cloves, thinly sliced**

In a large glass jar with a tight-fitting lid, combine the first six ingredients. Add the mushrooms, onion and garlic. Cover and shake gently to coat. Refrigerate for 8 hours or overnight. Drain before serving.

RASPBERRY CHIPOTLE GLAZE FOR HAM

Add something new to your traditional ham entree with this simple glaze. It covers an 8- to 10-pound ham and provides about 20 servings.

—MARY LOU WAYMAN SALT LAKE CITY, UT

START TO FINISH: 15 MIN.
MAKES: 1⅔ CUPS (ENOUGH FOR AN 8- TO 10-POUND HAM)

- **1 jar (12 ounces) seedless raspberry jam**
- **2 tablespoons white vinegar**
- **2 chipotle peppers in adobo sauce, drained, seeded and minced**
- **2 to 3 garlic cloves, minced**
- **2 teaspoons coarsely ground pepper**

In a small saucepan, combine the jam, vinegar, peppers and garlic. Bring to a boil. Reduce heat; simmer, uncovered, 5 minutes. Brush over ham during the last 30 minutes of cooking. Sprinkle with pepper before serving.

BARBECUE SAUCE WITH MUSTARD

START TO FINISH: 20 MIN.
MAKES: 4 CUPS

- ½ **cup sugar**
- ¼ **teaspoon ground oregano**
- ½ **teaspoon ground thyme**
- 1 **teaspoon salt**
- ½ **teaspoon pepper**
- ⅛ **teaspoon cayenne pepper**
- ½ **teaspoon cornstarch**
- ½ **cup vinegar**
- 1 **cup molasses**
- 1 **cup ketchup**
- 1 **cup prepared mustard**
- 2 **tablespoons canola oil**

1. Combine first seven ingredients in a small saucepan. Stir in enough vinegar to make a paste. Combine molasses, ketchup, mustard, oil and remaining vinegar; add to herb paste. Bring to a boil, stirring constantly. Reduce heat and simmer 10 minutes. Remove from heat; cool completely.
2. Pour into a glass jar; cover tightly. Store refrigerated up to 3 months. Baste over smoked chicken, turkey, ham or hot dogs.

> Say no to ho-hum barbecue. Add some zing to chicken or pork with our sauce.
>
> **—CHARLIE AND RUTHIE KNOTE**
> CAPE GIRARDEAU, MO

SPICY MUSTARD

When I make this mustard, I add fresh horseradish from our garden and vinegar seasoned with homegrown tarragon. It adds a little extra zip to burgers and sandwiches.

—**JOYCE LONSDALE** UNIONVILLE, PA

PREP: 15 MIN.
COOK: 5 MIN. + STANDING
MAKES: 1½ CUPS

- ½ **cup tarragon or cider vinegar**
- ½ **cup water**
- ¼ **cup olive oil**
- 2 **tablespoons prepared horseradish**
- ½ **teaspoon lemon juice**
- 1 **cup ground mustard**
- ½ **cup sugar**
- ½ **teaspoon salt**

1. In a blender or food processor, combine all ingredients; cover and process 1 minute. Scrape down the sides of the container and process for 30 seconds.

2. Transfer to a small saucepan and let stand 10 minutes. Cook over low heat until bubbly, stirring constantly. Cool completely. If a thinner mustard is desired, stir in an additional 1-2 tablespoons water. Pour the mustard into small airtight containers. Store in the refrigerator.

WASABI BUTTER

A hint of wasabi's mustard-horseradish flavor makes the sweet taste of corn pop. It's just as tasty smeared over cornbread.

—**NILA GRAHL** GURNEE, IL

START TO FINISH: 5 MIN.
MAKES: ½ CUP

- ½ **cup butter, softened**
- 1 **tablespoon chopped green onion (green part only)**
- 1½ **teaspoons prepared wasabi**
- ¼ **teaspoon reduced-sodium soy sauce**

In a small bowl, beat all ingredients. Refrigerate up to 1 week or freeze up to 3 months.

CURRY MAYO DIPPING SAUCE

Curry powder and hot pepper sauce lend bold flavor and a little kick to this fantastic dipping sauce.

—**JOAN HALLFORD** FORT WORTH, TX

PREP: 5 MIN. + CHILLING
MAKES: ABOUT 1 CUP

- 1 **cup mayonnaise**
- 3 **tablespoons 2% milk**
- 5 **teaspoons curry powder**
- ¼ **teaspoon hot pepper sauce**

In a small bowl, combine all ingredients. Refrigerate for at least 1 hour.

THREE-PEPPER CHUTNEY

This sweet chutney is as tasty on pork, beef and poultry as it is on grilled hot dogs and hamburgers. We like it best on sandwiches instead of high-fat mayonnaise.

—LISA LOUW NEWBERRY, FL

PREP: 30 MIN.
COOK: 1½ HOURS + CHILLING
MAKES: 2 CUPS

- 1½ **cups packed brown sugar**
- 1½ **cups cider vinegar**
- 3 **medium green peppers, chopped**
- 3 **medium sweet red peppers, chopped**
- 3 **jalapeno peppers, seeded and chopped**
- 1 **medium onion, chopped**
- 1 **teaspoon salt**

1. In a large saucepan, combine all ingredients. Bring to a boil. Reduce the heat; simmer, uncovered, for 1½ to 2 hours or until thickened. Cool.

2. Pour into a serving bowl. Cover and refrigerate 1-2 hours or until chilled.

NOTE *Wear disposable gloves when cutting hot peppers; the oils can burn skin. Avoid touching your face.*

When a recipe calls for just an onion, we usually reach for a yellow Spanish onion. But depending on the recipe, you may wish to try other types. Strong-flavored white onions are ideal for Mexican dishes. Raw red onions are often added to salads and sandwiches for their bite. And, for a less pronounced onion flavor, try a sweet onion.

PEACH CHILI SAUCE

I've been eating this tasty chili sauce since my childhood. Now I serve it to my guests.
—**BARBARA BATTEN** BLENHEIM, ON

PREP: 2¾ HOURS • **PROCESS:** 20 MIN.
MAKES: 5 PINTS

- 5 **pounds tomatoes (about 15 medium)**
- 3 **medium peaches (about 1½ pounds)**
- 3 **large sweet onions, chopped (about 6 cups)**
- 3 **medium pears, peeled and chopped (about 3 cups)**
- 2 **medium green peppers, chopped (about 1½ cups)**
- 2 **celery ribs, chopped**
- 2 **jalapeno peppers, seeded and cut into matchsticks**
- 3 **cups sugar**
- 2 **cups white vinegar**
- 3 **teaspoons salt**
- 1 **teaspoon mixed pickling spices**

1. Fill a Dutch oven two-thirds with water; bring to a boil. Cut a shallow X on the bottom of each tomato and peach. Using tongs, place the tomatoes and peaches, a few at a time, in boiling water for 30-60 seconds or just until skin at the X begins to loosen. Remove the tomatoes and peaches; immediately drop into ice water. Pull off skins with tip of a knife; discard skins.

2. Coarsely chop the tomatoes and peaches; place in a stockpot. Add the onions, pears, green peppers, celery, jalapenos, sugar, vinegar and salt. Place pickling spices on a double thickness of cheesecloth. Gather corners of cloth to enclose spices; tie securely with string.

Add to stockpot. Bring to a boil. Reduce heat; simmer, uncovered, 2 to 2½ hours or until thickened, stirring occasionally. Discard spice bag.

3. Carefully ladle hot mixture into five hot 1-pint jars, leaving ½-in. headspace. Remove the air bubbles and adjust headspace, if necessary, by adding hot mixture. Wipe rims. Center lids on jars; screw on bands until fingertip tight.

4. Place the jars into canner with simmering water, ensuring that they are completely covered with water. Bring to a boil; process for 20 minutes. Remove jars and cool.

NOTE *Wear disposable gloves when cutting hot peppers; the oils can burn skin. Avoid touching your face. The processing time listed is for altitudes of 1,000 feet or less. For altitudes up to 3,000 feet, add 5 minutes; 6,000 feet, add 10 minutes; 8,000 feet, add 15 minutes; 10,000 feet, add 20 minutes.*

CHILI SEAFOOD SAUCE

My husband and I like to treat ourselves to a shrimp appetizer twice a month. Our favorite way to eat shrimp is with this sauce.
—**ALYCE WYMAN** PEMBINA, ND

START TO FINISH: 5 MIN.
MAKES: 1 CUP

- ½ **cup ketchup**
- ½ **cup chili sauce**
- 1 **tablespoon lemon juice**
- 1 **tablespoon prepared horseradish**
- ⅛ **teaspoon hot pepper sauce**

In a small bowl, combine the ketchup, chili sauce, lemon juice, horseradish and pepper sauce. Cover and refrigerate until serving.

TRIPLE BERRY SALSA

START TO FINISH: 20 MIN.
MAKES: 22 SERVINGS (¼ CUP EACH)

- 1½ cups fresh blueberries
- ¾ cup chopped fresh strawberries
- ¾ cup fresh raspberries
- 1 medium tomato, seeded and chopped
- 1 small sweet yellow pepper, chopped
- ¼ cup finely chopped red onion
- ¼ cup minced fresh cilantro
- 1 jalapeno pepper, seeded and minced
- 2 green onions, chopped
- 1 tablespoon cider vinegar
- 1 tablespoon olive oil
- 2 teaspoons lime juice
- 2 teaspoons orange juice
- 1 teaspoon honey
- ¼ teaspoon salt
  Baked tortilla chip scoops

In a large bowl, mix first nine ingredients. In a small bowl, whisk the vinegar, oil, juices, honey and salt. Drizzle over salsa; toss to coat. Chill until serving. Serve with chips.

NOTE *Wear disposable gloves when cutting hot peppers; the oils can burn skin. Avoid touching your face.*

Blueberries are so nutritious, low in calories and packed with vitamin C, fiber and disease-fighting antioxidants. This chunky salsa is a fresh, flavorful blend of berries and veggies and would be great over grilled chicken, too.
—**RAYMONDE BOURGEOIS** SWASTIKA, ON

EASY RHUBARB RELISH

I remember eating this relish at my grandmother's over 50 years ago. My mother made it for years and now my daughters make it. It complements any meat, but I find it a must with meat loaf.

—HELEN BROOKS LACOMBE, AB

PREP: 10 MIN.
COOK: 2 HOURS + CHILLING
MAKES: 4 PINTS

- **12 cups finely chopped fresh or frozen rhubarb**
- **1 medium onion, chopped**
- **2 cups sugar**
- **1 cup cider vinegar**
- **1 teaspoon salt**
- **1 teaspoon ground cloves**
- **1 teaspoon ground allspice**
- **¼ teaspoon paprika**
- **1 teaspoon ground cinnamon**

1. Rinse four 2-cup plastic containers and lids with boiling water. Dry the containers and lids thoroughly.

2. In a large saucepan, combine all ingredients. Bring to a boil. Reduce heat and simmer about 2 hours or until mixture thickens, stirring occasionally.

3. Fill all containers to within ½ in. of tops. Wipe off top edges of containers; cover with lids. Refrigerate for up to 3 weeks or freeze extra containers up to 12 months. Thaw frozen relish in refrigerator before serving.

DR PEPPER BBQ SAUCE

My family is stationed in Italy with my husband, Lieutenant William Robert Blackman. William grew up in Memphis and I'm from Texas, so the dish that spells "home" for us is barbecue. I have my own recipe for barbecue sauce that we like to pour all over sliced brisket. Eating it reminds us of weekend barbecues with our families.

—TINA BLACKMAN NAPLES, AE

PREP: 5 MIN. • **COOK:** 35 MIN.
MAKES: 1 CUP

- 1 can (12 ounces) Dr Pepper
- 1 cup crushed tomatoes
- ¼ cup packed brown sugar
- 2 tablespoons spicy brown mustard
- 1 tablespoon orange juice
- 1 tablespoon Worcestershire sauce
- 1 garlic clove, minced
- ¼ teaspoon salt
- ⅛ teaspoon pepper

In a small saucepan, combine all the ingredients; bring to a boil. Reduce heat; simmer, uncovered, 30-35 minutes or until slightly thickened, stirring occasionally. Refrigerate leftovers.

HOMEMADE PIZZA SAUCE

PREP: 10 MIN. • **COOK:** 70 MIN.
MAKES: ABOUT 4 CUPS

- **2** cans (15 ounces each) tomato sauce
- **1** can (12 ounces) tomato paste
- **1** tablespoon Italian seasoning
- **1** tablespoon dried oregano
- **1** to 2 teaspoons fennel seed, crushed
- **1** teaspoon onion powder
- **1** teaspoon garlic powder
- **½** teaspoon salt

1. Rinse four 1-cup plastic containers and lids with boiling water. Dry the containers and lids thoroughly.
2. In a large saucepan over medium heat, combine tomato sauce and paste. Add remaining ingredients; mix well. Bring to a boil, stirring constantly. Reduce heat; cover and simmer for 1 hour, stirring occasionally. Cool.
3. Fill all containers to within ½ in. of tops. Wipe off top edges of container. Freeze up to 12 months. Thaw frozen sauce in refrigerator before serving.
NOTE *Use the sauce with crust and toppings of your choice to make a pizza; 1⅓ cups of sauce will cover a crust in a 15x10x1-in. pan.*

> For years, I had trouble finding a pizza my family liked, so I started making my own pizza. When I prepare my sauce, I usually fix enough of it for three to four pizzas and freeze it.
> —**CHERYL KRAVIK** SPANAWAY, WA

FOOD TRIVIA!
Pizza is here to stay! According to the USDA, every day about one-eighth of Americans will have a slice of pizza.

SPICY BAVARIAN BEER MUSTARD

Here's a gift that has bite! Include a festive tag that lists serving suggestions. For example, the spicy beer mustard is great with pretzels.
—*TASTE OF HOME* TEST KITCHEN

PREP: 15 MIN. + CHILLING
PROCESS: 15 MIN.
MAKES: 7 HALF-PINTS

- 2 **cups dark beer**
- 2 **cups brown mustard seed**
- 2 **cups ground mustard**
- 1½ **cups packed brown sugar**
- 1½ **cups malt vinegar**
- ½ **cup balsamic vinegar**
- 3 **teaspoons salt**
- 2 **teaspoons ground allspice**
- ½ **teaspoon ground cloves**
- 2 **teaspoons vanilla extract**

1. In a bowl, mix beer and mustard seeds. Cover; refrigerate overnight.

2. Place seed mixture in a blender. Cover and process until chopped and slightly grainy. Transfer to a Dutch oven. Add the ground mustard, brown sugar, vinegars, salt, allspice and cloves. Bring just to a boil. Remove from heat; stir in vanilla.

3. Ladle hot liquid into seven hot half-pint jars, leaving ½-in. headspace. Wipe rims. Center lids on jars; screw on bands until fingertip tight.

4. Place the jars into canner with simmering water, ensuring that they are completely covered with water. Bring to a boil; process for 10 minutes. Remove jars and cool.

NOTE *The processing time listed is for altitudes of 1,000 feet or less. For altitudes up to 3,000 feet, add 5 minutes; 6,000 feet, add 10 minutes; 8,000 feet, add 15 minutes; 10,000 feet, add 20 minutes.*

I threw this together after an overzealous trip to the farmer's market! My family loved it from the first bite. You can serve it right away, but the best flavor is achieved after letting the salsa rest in the refrigerator for a few hours. **—ANDREA HEYART** AUBREY, TX

WATERMELON SALSA

START TO FINISH: 25 MIN.
MAKES: 15 SERVINGS (⅓ CUP EACH)

- ¼ **cup lime juice**
- 3 **tablespoons brown sugar**
- 2 **tablespoons cider vinegar**
- 1 **tablespoon honey**
- ¼ **teaspoon salt**
- 3 **cups seeded chopped watermelon**
- 1 **medium cucumber, seeded and chopped**
- 1 **small red onion, finely chopped**
- 2 **jalapeno peppers, seeded and finely chopped**
- ¼ **cup finely chopped sweet yellow pepper**
- ¼ **cup minced fresh cilantro**
- 2 **tablespoons minced fresh basil**

In a large bowl, combine the first five ingredients. Add the remaining ingredients; then toss to combine. Refrigerate, covered, until serving. If necessary, drain before serving.

NOTE *Wear disposable gloves when cutting hot peppers; the oils can burn skin. Avoid touching your face.*

FOOD TRIVIA!
While watermelon is used as a fruit, it's technically a vegetable.
Watermelons are related to cucumbers and squash. Watermelons can be round or oblong, with red or yellow flesh. Seedless watermelons are not really seedless; they just have fewer seeds, which are edible.

GREEN ONION TARTAR SAUCE

Here's a traditional sauce worth making from scratch. It makes the meal feel very special, and guests are always impressed. You might never buy the bottled stuff again.
—**ROGER SLIVON** GENESEE DEPOT, WI

START TO FINISH: 10 MIN.
MAKES: ¾ CUP

- ½ **cup mayonnaise**
- 2 **green onions, finely chopped**
- 1 **whole dill pickle, finely chopped**
- 2 **tablespoons sour cream**
- 1 **teaspoon minced fresh parsley**
- 1 **teaspoon cider vinegar**
- ½ **teaspoon sugar**
- ¼ **teaspoon dried tarragon**
- ⅛ **teaspoon pepper**

In a small bowl, combine all the ingredients. Refrigerate until serving.

CRISP ONION RELISH

I take this relish to picnics for people to use as a condiment on hamburgers and hot dogs. It adds a special zing!

—MARIE PATKAU HANLEY, SK

PREP: 10 MIN. + CHILLING
MAKES: ABOUT 6 CUPS

- **4 medium sweet onions, halved and thinly sliced**
- **½ cup sugar**
- **⅓ cup water**
- **⅓ cup cider vinegar**
- **1 cup mayonnaise**
- **1 teaspoon celery seed**

Place onions in a large bowl. In a small bowl, combine the sugar, water and vinegar; stir until sugar is dissolved. Pour over onions. Cover and refrigerate at least 3 hours. Drain and discard liquid from onions. Combine mayonnaise and celery seed; add to onions and mix well. Store in the refrigerator.

SWEET & SPICY BARBECUE SAUCE

I've never cared that much for store-bought barbecue sauce. I prefer to make things myself from scratch including this spicy, deep red-brown sauce. You'll find it clings well when you slather it on grilled meat.

—HELENA GEORGETTE MANN
SACRAMENTO, CA

PREP: 30 MIN. • **COOK:** 35 MIN.
MAKES: 1½ CUPS

- 1 **medium onion, chopped**
- 1 **tablespoon canola oil**
- 1 **garlic clove, minced**
- 1 **to 3 teaspoons chili powder**
- ¼ **teaspoon cayenne pepper**
- ¼ **teaspoon coarsely ground pepper**
- 1 **cup ketchup**
- ⅓ **cup molasses**
- 2 **tablespoons cider vinegar**
- 2 **tablespoons Worcestershire sauce**
- 2 **tablespoons spicy brown mustard**
- ½ **teaspoon hot pepper sauce**

1. In a saucepan, saute onion in oil until tender. Add garlic; cook 1 minute. Stir in the chili powder, cayenne and pepper; cook 1 minute longer.

2. Stir in the ketchup, molasses, vinegar, Worcestershire sauce, mustard and pepper sauce. Bring to a boil. Reduce heat; simmer, uncovered, for 30-40 minutes or until sauce reaches desired consistency. Cool 15 minutes.

3. Strain sauce through a fine mesh strainer over a large bowl, discarding vegetables and seasonings. Store in an airtight container in the refrigerator up to 1 month. Use as a basting sauce for grilled meats.

GINGERED PEAR & CURRANT CHUTNEY

We can our homegrown harvest. This spiced pear chutney is good with pork.

—ELLEN MOORE SPRINGFIELD, NH

PREP: 2¾ HOURS • **PROCESS:** 15 MIN.
MAKES: 6 PINTS

- 3 **cups sugar**
- 3 **cups cider vinegar**
- 2 **small lemons, thinly sliced and seeds removed**
- 1 **large onion, chopped**
- 1 **cup dried currants**
- ⅓ **cup minced fresh gingerroot**
- 2 **garlic cloves, minced**
- 1 **teaspoon ground allspice**
- 20 **large pears (about 6 pounds), peeled and chopped**

1. In a Dutch oven, bring the first eight ingredients to a boil; stir occasionally. Reduce heat; simmer, uncovered, 15-20 minutes or until syrupy. Stir in pears. Return to a boil. Reduce heat; simmer, uncovered, 1¾ hours or until fruit is tender and mixture is thickened; stir occasionally. Remove from heat.

2. Ladle hot mixture into six hot 1-pint jars, leaving ½-in. headspace. Remove air bubbles and adjust the headspace. Wipe rims. Center lids on jars; screw on bands until fingertip tight.

3. Place the jars into the canner with simmering water, ensuring that they are completely covered with water. Bring to a boil; process for 15 minutes. Remove jars and cool.

NOTE *The processing time listed is for altitudes of 1,000 feet or less. For altitudes up to 3,000 feet, add 5 minutes; 6,000 feet, add 10 minutes; 8,000 feet, add 15 minutes; 10,000 feet, add 20 minutes.*

TANGY PINEAPPLE GLAZE

Try something new this year with your traditional ham and this easy, tasty glaze. It will cover an 8- to 10-pound ham and provide about 20 servings.

—JOAN HALLFORD FORT WORTH, TX

START TO FINISH: 5 MIN.
MAKES: 1 CUP (ENOUGH FOR AN 8- TO 10-POUND HAM)

- 1 **can (8 ounces) unsweetened crushed pineapple, drained**
- ½ **cup apricot jam**
- 1 **tablespoon spicy brown mustard**
- 2 **teaspoons prepared horseradish**

In a small bowl, combine all ingredients. Brush over ham during the last 30 minutes of cooking.

I love impressing dinner guests with flavored butter. I mix up a big batch, and then freeze it so when company comes, this special spread is ready to go. Cut slices in different shapes for a little fun.

—PAM DUNCAN SUMMERS, AR

FRESH HERB BUTTER

PREP: 25 MIN. + FREEZING
MAKES: ABOUT 2 DOZEN

- 1 **cup butter, softened**
- 2 **tablespoons minced fresh chives**
- 2 **tablespoons minced fresh parsley**
- 1 **tablespoon minced fresh tarragon**
- 1 **tablespoon lemon juice**
- ¼ **teaspoon pepper**

1. In a small bowl, beat all ingredients until blended. Spread onto a baking sheet to ½-in. thickness. Freeze, covered, until firm.
2. Cut the butter with a 1-in. cookie cutter. Store, layered between waxed paper, in an airtight container in the refrigerator up to 1 week or in the freezer up to 3 months.

CURRY BUTTER

You'll love the earthy flavor curry lends to corn, but this butter is great with any veggie, potatoes included.
—ELKE ROSE WAUKESHA, WI

START TO FINISH: 5 MIN.
MAKES: ½ CUP

- ½ **cup butter, softened**
- 1½ **teaspoons curry powder**
- ½ **teaspoon ground cumin**
- ¼ **teaspoon crushed red pepper flakes**

In a small bowl, beat all ingredients. Refrigerate up to 1 week or freeze up to 3 months.

SWEET-HOT ASIAN DIPPING SAUCE

This Asian-inspired sauce makes a delicious dip for egg rolls or veggies. It can also be used to make a sweet-tangy vinaigrette.
—*TASTE OF HOME* TEST KITCHEN

PREP: 30 MIN. • **PROCESS:** 20 MIN.
MAKES: 6 HALF-PINTS

- 3 **cups sugar**
- 3 **cups cider vinegar**
- ¼ **cup crushed red pepper flakes**
- 6 **garlic cloves, minced**
- 2 **tablespoons minced fresh gingerroot**
- 1½ **teaspoons canning salt**

1. In a Dutch oven, bring sugar and vinegar to a boil. Reduce heat; simmer, uncovered, 5 minutes. Remove from heat; stir in the remaining ingredients.

2. Ladle hot liquid into six hot half-pint jars, leaving ¼-in. headspace. Wipe rims. Center lids on jars; screw on bands until fingertip tight.

3. Place the jars into canner with simmering water, ensuring that they are completely covered with water. Bring to a boil; process for 20 minutes. Remove jars and cool.

NOTE *The processing time listed is for altitudes of 1,000 feet or less. Add 1 minute to the processing time for each 1,000 feet of additional altitude. Serve dipping sauce with assorted fresh vegetables or your favorite hot appetizer. To make a vinaigrette, combine 1 part dipping sauce with 2 parts oil and toss with cut lettuce.*

Sweet Butters & Sauces

PEAR-ADISE BUTTER

Vanilla and rosemary accent this thick, smooth butter that positively shouts "pears" throughout. Spread some on ordinary bread and you'll have a fruity feast.

—KRISTINA PONTIER HILLSBORO, OR

PREP: 15 MIN. • **COOK:** 2 HOURS + CHILLING
MAKES: 2 CUPS

- 4 **cups pear juice**
- 4 **pounds pears, peeled and cut into 1-inch pieces**
- ¼ **teaspoon salt**
- 1 **vanilla bean (3 inches), split in half lengthwise**
- 3 **fresh rosemary sprigs (4 inches)**
- 1 **teaspoon white balsamic vinegar**

1. In a large saucepan, bring pear juice to a boil; cook 30 minutes or until reduced to 1 cup. Stir in pears and salt; return to a boil. Reduce heat; cover and cook 15-20 minutes or until pears are tender. Cool slightly.

2. Transfer pear mixture to a food processor; cover and process until smooth. Return to the pan; add vanilla bean. Bring to a boil over medium heat, stirring constantly. Reduce heat; simmer, uncovered, 65-75 minutes or until thickened, stirring occasionally.

3. Remove from heat. Discard the vanilla bean. Stir in rosemary and vinegar; cover and let stand 30 minutes.

4. Discard rosemary. Cool to room temperature. Cover and refrigerate the butter at least 4 hours before serving.

STICKY NOTES

CHUNKY FRUIT AND NUT RELISH

I tuck a large glass jar of this colorful condiment alongside the fudge and cookies in my holiday baskets. Packed with pecans, the fruit relish is delicious served with ham or poultry.

—DONNA BROCKETT KINGFISHER, OK

PREP: 5 MIN.
COOK: 10 MIN. + CHILLING
MAKES: 6 CUPS

- 2 **packages (12 ounces each) fresh or frozen cranberries**
- 1½ **cups sugar**
- 1 **cup orange juice**
- 1 **can (15¼ ounces) sliced peaches, drained and cut up**
- 1 **cup chopped pecans**
- ¾ **cup pineapple tidbits**
- ½ **cup golden raisins**

1. In a large saucepan, bring the cranberries, sugar and juice to a boil, stirring occasionally. Reduce heat; simmer, uncovered, for 8-10 minutes or until cranberries pop.
2. Remove from heat; stir in the peaches, pecans, pineapple and raisins. Cool. Cover and refrigerate at least 3 hours.

CHERRY BOUNCE

PREP: 5 MIN. • **COOK:** 25 MIN. + STANDING
MAKES: 5¼ CUPS

- 4½ **pounds fresh unpitted sweet cherries**
- 2¼ **cups sugar**
- ½ **teaspoon ground allspice**
- 1½ **cups spiced rum**
- 1½ **cups brandy**

1. Place cherries in a large saucepan. Bring to a boil. Reduce heat; simmer, uncovered, 15-20 minutes or until soft. Strain juice through a cheesecloth-lined colander; divide cherries among six 1-pint jars.
2. Return the juice to saucepan; add the sugar and allspice. Bring to a boil. Reduce heat; simmer, uncovered, 5 minutes. Transfer to a large bowl; cool completely.
3. Stir in rum and brandy; pour syrup into bottles over cherries. Cover and let stand at least 1 month, stirring every week. Store in a cool dry place up to 3 months.

FOOD TRIVIA!
Cherry Bounce dates back to Colonial times. It's made by fermenting fruit and spices in rum and brandy. It's said in 1792 a local tavern owner, Joel Lane, influenced North Carolina's state legislators to buy some of his land for the state capital by serving them Cherry Bounce.

Smooth and with the fragrant flavor of sweet cherries, this homemade libation makes a wonderful holiday gift. For an additional treat, the drained cherries are delicious over vanilla ice cream. —**MATT WARREN** MEQUON, WI

TART CRANBERRY BUTTER

One of my favorite toppings for toast is this tart spread. It's also great spooned over poultry...and ice cream! I frequently give jars as gifts and have always gotten positive comments in return.

—CAROL STUDEBAKER GLADSTONE, MO

PREP: 5 MIN. • **COOK:** 30 MIN. + CHILLING
MAKES: 5 CUPS

- **10 cups fresh or frozen cranberries**
- **⅔ cup apple juice**
- **½ to ¾ cup sugar**
- **1 cup maple syrup**
- **½ cup honey**
- **½ teaspoon ground cinnamon**

1. In a saucepan over medium heat, bring the cranberries, apple juice and sugar to a boil. Cook 10-15 minutes or until all berries have popped, stirring occasionally. Remove from heat; cool slightly. Process in batches in a blender or food processor until smooth.

2. Return cranberry mixture to the saucepan; add remaining ingredients. Bring mixture to a boil over medium heat. Reduce heat; simmer, uncovered, 10 minutes or until thickened, stirring occasionally. Cover and chill 8 hours or overnight. Store in an airtight container in the refrigerator up to 1 week or freeze up to 3 months.

ZESTY LEMON CURD

There are lemon trees in our backyard, so I'm always on the prowl for new ways to use the fruit. When we shared some of our homegrown citrus with neighbors—Canadians who were spending the winter here—the wife repaid us by giving us this recipe! The curd keeps well, and it can be used for any meal. It's a great dessert topping on plain cake or ice cream.

—JEAN GAINES BULLHEAD CITY, AZ

PREP: 5 MIN. • **COOK:** 20 MIN. + COOLING
MAKES: 3 CUPS

- 3 **eggs, lightly beaten**
- 2 **cups sugar**
- ¾ **cup lemon juice**
- 2 **teaspoons grated lemon peel**
- 1 **cup butter, cubed**

1. In a large heavy saucepan, whisk the eggs, sugar, lemon juice and peel until blended. Add butter; cook over medium heat, whisking constantly, until mixture is thick enough to coat the back of a metal spoon and a thermometer reads at least 170°. Do not allow to boil. Remove from heat immediately. Transfer to a small bowl; cool. Press the plastic wrap onto the surface of curd. Refrigerate until cold.

2. Spread on muffins or rolls, or serve over waffles or ice cream.

FOOD TRIVIA!

Lemon curd is a thick, sweetly tart custard. Curd can be used as a spread on scones or slices of toast, as a topping for gingerbread and a filling for pies or cakes.

BUTTERNUT SQUASH BUTTER

PREP: 20 MIN. • **COOK:** 1 HOUR
MAKES: 6 CUPS

- 6 **cups mashed cooked butternut squash or pumpkin**
- 2 **cups apple cider or juice**
- 1¼ **cups packed brown sugar**
- 1 **teaspoon ground cinnamon**
- ½ **teaspoon ground ginger**
- ½ **teaspoon ground nutmeg**
- ⅛ **teaspoon ground cloves**

Place all ingredients in a Dutch oven. Bring to a boil. Reduce heat; simmer, uncovered, 1 to 1½ hours or until mixture reaches a thick, spreadable consistency. Cool to room temperature. Store in an airtight container the refrigerator up to 3 weeks.

Looking for a tasty way to use up pumpkins and have a wonderful gift during the holidays? My squash butter is delicious on biscuits or homemade bread, and it also makes a tempting filling for miniature tart shells.

—**WANDA RICHARDSON** SOMERS, MT

PLUM APPLE BUTTER

Use the season's freshest fruits to create your own spread for breads and crackers. The creamy, fruity butter is perfect for a warm summer day.

—NANCY MICHEL LAKELAND, FL

PREP: 10 MIN.
COOK: 35 MIN. + COOLING
MAKES: 1¼ CUPS

- 3 **medium fresh plums, pitted and quartered**
- 2 **medium tart apples, peeled and quartered**
- ¼ **cup water**
- ¾ **cup sugar**
- ¼ **to ½ teaspoon ground cinnamon**
- ¼ **teaspoon ground nutmeg**
  Dash ground allspice

1. Place plums, apples and water in a large saucepan. Bring to a boil. Reduce heat; cover and simmer 12-15 minutes or until tender. Cool slightly.
2. Place in a blender; cover and process until pureed. Return all to the saucepan. Add sugar and spices; return to a boil. Reduce the heat; simmer, uncovered, 15-20 minutes or until thickened, stirring frequently.
3. Cool to room temperature. Store in an airtight container in the refrigerator up to 3 weeks.

MOCHA CASHEW BUTTER

Flavored with coffee, chocolate and cashews, this easy-to-make spread is a yummy alternative to peanut butter.

—MARY HOUCHIN LEBANON, IL

START TO FINISH: 25 MIN.
MAKES: 2¼ CUPS

- 3 **cups salted cashews**
- ½ **cup butter, softened, divided**
- ½ **cup semisweet chocolate chips**
- 2 **teaspoons instant coffee granules**
- 2 **teaspoons water**
  Additional salted cashews, optional

1. Place cashews in a food processor. Cover and process until finely ground. Add ¼ cup butter; process until smooth. Transfer to a small bowl.
2. In a small saucepan, combine the chocolate chips, coffee granules, water and remaining butter. Cook and stir over low heat until smooth. Stir into the cashew mixture. If desired, top with additional cashews. Store in the refrigerator.

BLOOD ORANGE CURD

Blood oranges give this curd a unique color. You can use it as a substitute for lemon curd.

—TASTE OF HOME TEST KITCHEN

PREP: 35 MIN. + CHILLING • **MAKES:** 1⅓ CUPS

- 3 **eggs**
- 1 **cup sugar**
- ½ **cup blood orange juice**
- 1 **tablespoon grated blood orange peel**
- ¼ **cup butter, cubed**
  Red food coloring, optional
  Gingersnap cookies

1. In a small heavy saucepan over medium heat, whisk the eggs, sugar, orange juice and peel until blended. Add butter; cook, whisking constantly, until mixture is thickened and coats the back of a metal spoon and a thermometer reads at least 170°. Do not allow to boil. Remove from heat immediately.

2. Transfer to a small bowl and tint with food coloring if desired. Cool 10 minutes. Cover and refrigerate until chilled. Serve with cookies.

PLUM SAUCE

This sauce easily makes any Asian dish simply mouthwatering. And the bonus is that you won't need a lot of extra time to prepare the recipe.

—DORIS CHAMBERLAIN SOUTH WEYMOUTH, MA

START TO FINISH: 15 MIN. • **MAKES:** 1 CUP

- ½ **cup plum preserves**
- ¼ **cup finely chopped onion**
- ¼ **cup apricot preserves**
- 2 **tablespoons brown sugar**
- 2 **tablespoons apple cider or juice**
- 2 **tablespoons soy sauce**
- 2 **tablespoons ketchup**
- 1 **garlic clove, minced**

In a small saucepan, combine all ingredients. Cook, stirring occasionally, over low heat to allow flavors to blend.

RASPBERRY BUTTER

This butter will really perk up a brunch buffet that includes homemade breads.

—HELEN LAMB SEYMOUR, MO

START TO FINISH: 5 MIN.
MAKES: ABOUT ¾ CUP

- ½ **cup butter, softened**
- ⅓ **cup fresh or frozen raspberries**
- 2 **tablespoons confectioners' sugar**
  Dash lemon juice

In a small bowl, combine all ingredients. Serve immediately. Store leftovers in the refrigerator.

SPICED APPLESAUCE

Cardamom and mace add a bit of unusual spicy flavor to this homemade applesauce. This dish is a wonderful way to make use of autumn's apple bounty.

—JANET THOMAS MCKEES ROCKS, PA

PREP: 20 MIN. • **COOK:** 30 MIN.
MAKES: 9 CUPS

- 6 **pounds tart apples (about 18 medium), peeled and quartered**
- 1 **cup apple cider or juice**
- ¾ **cup sugar**
- 2 **tablespoons lemon juice**
- 1 **cinnamon sticks (3 inches)**
- 1 **teaspoon ground ginger**
- 1 **teaspoon vanilla extract**
- ½ **teaspoon ground nutmeg**
- ½ **teaspoon ground mace**
- ¼ **to ½ teaspoon ground cardamom**

Place all ingredients in a Dutch oven. Cover and cook over medium-low heat 30-40 minutes or until the apples are tender, stirring occasionally. Remove from heat; discard the cinnamon stick. Mash the apples to desired consistency. Serve warm or cold. Store in an airtight container in the refrigerator.

CRANBERRY HONEY BUTTER

If you are traveling to a friend or loved one's home for the holidays, bring them something even better than a bottle of wine. My butter is a flavorful treat!

—ARISA CUPP WARREN, OR

START TO FINISH: 10 MIN.
MAKES: 24 SERVINGS

- 1 cup butter, softened
- ⅓ cup finely chopped dried cranberries
- ¼ cup honey
- 2 teaspoons grated orange peel
- ⅛ teaspoon kosher salt

In a small bowl, beat all ingredients until blended. Store in an airtight container in the refrigerator up to 2 weeks or freeze up to 3 months.

BERRY COMPOTE TOPPING

This sweet, fruity topping is fantastic served over toasted slices of pound cake as well as warm-from-the-oven biscuits! Try it over ice cream, too!

—WANDA WEDEKINDS
WEST FRANKFORT, IL

START TO FINISH: 20 MIN.
MAKES: 6 CUPS

- 1 cup sugar
- ⅓ cup cornstarch
- 1 cup cold water
- ½ cup lemon juice
- ½ cup maple syrup
- 4 cups fresh strawberries, halved
- 2 cups fresh raspberries
- 2 cups fresh blackberries

1. In a large saucepan, combine sugar and cornstarch. Stir in water, lemon juice and syrup until smooth. Stir in berries. Bring to a boil over medium heat; cook and stir 2 minutes or until thickened.
2. Serve immediately or transfer to freezer containers. May be frozen up to 3 months.
3. To use frozen sauce, thaw in the refrigerator overnight. Place in a saucepan and heat through.

BILL'S APPLE BUTTER

Since retiring, I have more time to tend to our 75 apple trees and to experiment in the kitchen. I came up with this old-fashioned apple butter after some trial and error. The Red Hots make it unique.

—**BILL ELLIOTT** URBANA, MO

PREP: 3½ HOURS • **PROCESS:** 5 MIN.
MAKES: 8 PINTS

- **15 pounds early-season apples (Gala, Jonathan and/or Cortland), peeled and quartered**
- **¾ cup cider vinegar**
- **5⅓ cups packed brown sugar**
- **4 cups sugar**
- **2 tablespoons ground cinnamon**
- **1 teaspoon salt**
- **1 teaspoon cinnamon extract**
- **½ teaspoon ground cloves**
- **½ teaspoon ground allspice**
- **1 cup Red Hots**
- **1 cup boiling water**

1. In a stockpot, combine apples and vinegar; bring to a boil. Reduce heat; simmer, uncovered, 30-40 minutes or until tender. Remove from heat; cool slightly. Process in batches in a food processor until blended. Return all to pan.

2. Add sugars, cinnamon, salt, extract, cloves and allspice. Dissolve Red Hots in boiling water; stir into apple mixture.

3. Bring to a boil. Reduce heat; simmer, uncovered, 2 hours or until mixture reaches a thick, spreadable consistency.

4. Remove from heat. Carefully ladle hot mixture into eight hot sterilized 1-pint jars, leaving ¼-in. headspace. Remove the air bubbles and adjust headspace, if necessary, by adding hot mixture. Wipe rims. Center lids on jars; screw on bands until fingertip tight.

5. Place the jars into canner with simmering water, ensuring that they are completely covered with water. Bring to a boil; process for 5 minutes. Remove jars and cool.

NOTE *The processing time listed is for altitudes of 1,000 feet or less. Add 1 minute to the processing time for each 1,000 feet of additional altitude.*

SWEET-AND-SOUR SAUCE

You won't want to buy bottled sweet-and-sour sauce from the store after sampling this tongue-tingling recipe. It goes together in mere moments and requires only a handful of ingredients.

—**FLO WEISS** SEASIDE, OR

START TO FINISH: 5 MIN.
MAKES: ⅔ CUP

- **½ cup orange marmalade**
- **2 tablespoons white vinegar**
- **1 tablespoon diced pimientos**
- **⅛ teaspoon paprika**
  Dash salt

Combine all ingredients in a small bowl; cover and refrigerate until serving.

FIVE-FRUIT COMPOTE

Bring out the best in your Easter ham or lamb with this fast fruit compote.

—JEAN ECOS HARTLAND, WI

START TO FINISH: 20 MIN.
MAKES: 6 CUPS

- **2 cans (15 ounces each) sliced peaches in juice, drained**
- **1 can (20 ounces) unsweetened pineapple chunks, drained**
- **1 can (20 ounces) reduced-sugar cherry pie filling**
- **⅔ cup chopped dried apricots**
- **⅔ cup chopped dates**
- **½ teaspoon ground cinnamon**
  Fully cooked lean ham

In a large saucepan, combine first six ingredients. Bring to a boil. Reduced heat. Simmer, uncovered, 5 minutes; stir frequently. Serve warm with ham.

BLUEBERRY-RHUBARB BREAKFAST SAUCE

Here is my family's favorite breakfast topping. Sometimes I'll substitute cherry pie filling for the blueberry pie filling—it makes a tasty sauce, too!

—RITA WAGENMANN GRANGEVILLE, ID

START TO FINISH: 30 MIN.
MAKES: 7 CUPS

- **6 cups finely chopped rhubarb**
- **4 cups sugar**
- **1 can (21 ounces) blueberry pie filling**
- **1 package (3 ounces) raspberry gelatin**

1. Rinse seven 1-cup plastic containers and lids with boiling water. Dry the containers and lids thoroughly.

2. In a saucepan, bring rhubarb and sugar to a boil. Boil 10 minutes. Remove from heat; add pie filling and mix well. Bring to a boil. Remove from heat and stir in gelatin.

3. Fill all containers to within ½ in. of tops. Wipe off top edges of containers; cover with lids.

4. Refrigerate up to 3 weeks or freeze up to 12 months. Thaw frozen jam in refrigerator before serving. Serve with pancakes, waffles or toast.

ROSE PETAL HONEY

PREP: 5 MIN. • **COOK:** 35 MIN. + COOLING
MAKES: ABOUT 1 CUP

- 1 **cup packed rose petals (about 6 medium roses)**
- 1 **cup water**
- 2 **tablespoons lemon juice**
- 6 **tablespoons sugar**
- 1 **pouch (3 ounces) liquid fruit pectin**

1. In a large saucepan, combine rose petals, water and lemon juice; bring to a boil. Reduce heat; simmer, uncovered, until petals lose their color. Strain, reserving liquid and discarding petals. Return liquid to the saucepan.

2. Stir in sugar. Bring to a full rolling boil over high heat, stirring constantly. Stir in pectin. Continue to boil 1 minute, stirring constantly. Pour into a jar and cool to room temperature. Cover and refrigerate up to 3 weeks.

NOTE *Verify that flowers are edible and have not been treated with chemicals.*

When you want to serve a delicious but unique spread for scones or English muffins try this one. It is so simple to make and will impress guests at tea.
—**MARY KAY DIXSON**
DECATUR, AL

FOOD TRIVIA!
There are several edible flowers that add color and interest to a meal. Roses, borages, nasturtiums, violets and calendulas add there own unique taste to salads, jellies and vinaigrettes. Before using, always verify that the flowers are indeed edible and not treated with chemicals.

PUMPKIN BUTTER

Biting into this spiced butter on a hot biscuit is absolutely heavenly. With a dash of whipped cream, you might think you're eating a slice of pumpkin pie!

—**JUNE BARRUS** SPRINGVILLE, UT

PREP: 5 MIN. • **COOK:** 20 MIN. + COOLING
MAKES: 6 CUPS

- 3 cans (15 ounces each) solid-pack pumpkin
- 2 cups sugar
- 1½ cups water
- 3 tablespoons lemon juice
- 1 tablespoon grated lemon peel
- 3 teaspoons ground cinnamon
- ¾ teaspoon salt
- ¾ teaspoon ground nutmeg
- ¾ teaspoon ground ginger

1. In a large saucepan, combine all ingredients. Bring to a boil, stirring frequently. Reduce heat; cover and simmer for 20 minutes to allow the flavors to blend.

2. Cool. Spoon into jars. Cover and store in the refrigerator for up to 3 weeks.

Morton Illinois calls itself the Pumpkin Capital of the world! Morton is home to the pumpkin processing plant for Libby's where about 85 percent of the world pumpkins are processed. Many of the pumpkins used are grown in the nearby Peoria area.

RASPBERRY CURD

Raspberries are such a sweet and flavorful berry that are perfect during the summer. This recipe can also be made in the winter with frozen berries.

—*TASTE OF HOME* TEST KITCHEN

PREP: 5 MIN. • **COOK:** 10 MIN. + CHILLING
MAKES: ¾ CUP

- 1⅔ to 2 cups fresh or frozen unsweetened raspberries
- ½ cup sugar
- 1 tablespoon cornstarch
- 2 tablespoons butter
- 3 egg yolks

1. Sieve raspberries through a strainer, pressing with the back of a spoon; reserve ½ cup 1 tablespoon juice. Discard seeds.

2. In a saucepan, combine sugar and cornstarch; add raspberry juice and butter. Cook and stir until thick and bubbly. In a small bowl, beat egg yolks until well blended. Stir in half of the raspberry mixture. Return all to the saucepan; bring to a gently boil. Cook and stir 2 minutes.

3. Place into small jars; place plastic wrap on surface of curd. Cover and chill. Store in the refrigerator.

BOURBON CRANBERRIES

Bourbon adds bite to this classic holiday standby. For gift-giving, wrap in a vintage tea towel or cloth napkin, cinch with ribbon and adorn with small ornaments.

—BECKY JO SMITH KETTLE FALLS, WA

PREP: 35 MIN. • **PROCESS:** 15 MIN.
MAKES: 4 HALF-PINTS

- 2 **packages (12 ounces each) fresh or frozen cranberries, thawed**
- 1½ **cups sugar**
- 1 **cup orange juice**
- ¼ **cup bourbon**
- 3 **teaspoons vanilla extract**
- 1 **teaspoon grated orange peel**

1. In a large saucepan, combine the cranberries, sugar, orange juice and bourbon. Bring to a boil. Reduce heat; simmer, uncovered, 18-22 minutes or until berries pop and the mixture has thickened.

2. Remove from heat. Stir in vanilla and orange peel. Ladle hot mixture into four hot half-pint jars, leaving ¼-in. headspace. Remove air bubbles and adjust headspace, if necessary, by adding hot mixture. Wipe the rims. Center lids on the jars; screw on the bands until fingertip tight.

3. Place the jars into canner with simmering water, ensuring that they are completely covered with water. Bring to a boil; process for 15 minutes. Remove jars and cool.

NOTE *The processing time listed is for altitudes of 1,000 feet or less. Add 1 minute to the processing time for each 1,000 feet of additional altitude.*

OLD-FASHIONED PEACH BUTTER

Cinnamon and ground cloves add homey flavor to this spread. Using the slow cooker eliminates much of the stirring required when simmering fruit butter on the stovetop.
—**MARILOU ROBINSON** PORTLAND, OR

PREP: 10 MIN.
COOK: 9 HOURS + COOLING
MAKES: 9 CUPS

- **14 cups coarsely chopped peeled fresh or frozen peaches (about 5½ pounds)**
- **2½ cups sugar**
- **4½ teaspoons lemon juice**
- **1½ teaspoons ground cinnamon**
- **¾ teaspoon ground cloves**
- **½ cup quick-cooking tapioca**

1. In a large bowl, combine the peaches, sugar, lemon juice, cinnamon and cloves. Transfer to a 5-qt. slow cooker. Cover and cook on low for 8-10 hours or until peaches are very soft, stirring occasionally.

2. Stir in tapioca. Cook, uncovered, on high 1 hour or until thickened. Pour into jars or freezer containers; cool to room temperature, about 1 hour. Cover and refrigerate up to 3 weeks or freeze up to 1 year.

SWEET HONEY ALMOND BUTTER

This homemade butter makes a nice gift along with bread fresh from the oven.
—**EVELYN HARRIS** WAYNESBORO, VA

START TO FINISH: 10 MIN.
MAKES: 2 CUPS

- **1 cup butter, softened**
- **¾ cup honey**
- **¾ cup confectioners' sugar**
- **¾ cup finely ground almonds**
- **¼ to ½ teaspoon almond extract**

In a bowl, combine all ingredients; mix well. Refrigerate up to 1 week or freeze up to 3 months.

| Vinegars & More |

CRANBERRY VINEGAR

For a delicious vinegar for salad dressings and marinades, try this vinegar with cranberries. It would be wonderful on a side salad during the holidays.

—LESLEY COLGAN LONDON, ON

START TO FINISH: 25 MIN.
MAKES: 1½ CUPS

- ¾ **cup white vinegar**
- ¾ **cup water**
- ¾ **cup sugar**
- 1 **cinnamon stick**
- 1 **package (12 ounces) fresh or frozen cranberries**

In a saucepan, bring all ingredients to a boil. Reduce heat and simmer for 5 minutes or until the cranberries burst. Cool. Strain through a fine sieve into sterilized bottles or jars. Seal tightly. Discard cranberries and cinnamon stick. Chill until ready to use.

NOTE *This cranberry-infused vinegar is delicious drizzled over roast pork or dipping baguette slices in it, too.*

FOOD TRIVIA!
Cranberries are one of a few fruits native to North America. In fact, we enjoy the ruby berries so much that we consume about 400 million pounds a year and over 80 million pounds during Thanksgiving alone!

HERBED GARLIC DIPPING OIL

Talk about versatility! This herb-infused oil has many uses. Spread over halved French bread and broil until toasted, toss with hot pasta, or simply use as a full-flavored dipping oil.

—DAWN EMBRY-RODRIGUEZ FLORENCE, CO

START TO FINISH: 20 MIN.
MAKES: 1 CUP PLUS 2 TABLESPOONS

- 1 **cup olive oil**
- 16 **to 20 fresh basil leaves**
- ¼ **cup minced fresh rosemary**
- 4 **teaspoons minced garlic**
- 1 **teaspoon salt**
- ⅓ **cup balsamic vinegar**
  Italian bread, cubed

Place the first five ingredients in a blender; cover and process until desired consistency. Transfer to a small bowl. Stir in vinegar. Serve with bread cubes.

HOMEMADE STRAWBERRY VINEGAR

Sweet and sour, this easy vinegar makes a great summer salad dressing.

—MARY HISE COCOA, FL

PREP: 20 MIN. + STANDING
COOK: 20 MIN. + COOLING
MAKES: 5 CUPS

- 4 **cups halved fresh strawberries**
- 4 **cups cider vinegar**
- 1 **cup sugar**

1. In a large bowl, mix the strawberries and vinegar. Cover and let stand for 1 hour. Transfer to a large saucepan. Stir in the sugar. Bring to a boil, stirring occasionally. Reduce the heat; cover and simmer 10 minutes. Remove from heat; cool completely.
2. Strain and discard pulp. Pour liquid into sterilized jars and cover. Store in a cool dark place.

OIL AND VINEGAR DRIZZLE

Use this on a classic sub with cheese, shredded lettuce and salami.

—TASTE OF HOME TEST KITCHEN

START TO FINISH: 10 MIN.
MAKES: ABOUT 5 TABLESPOONS

- 2 **tablespoons olive oil**
- 2 **tablespoons white wine vinegar**
- 1 **tablespoon grated Parmesan cheese**
- 1 **teaspoon sugar**
- ¼ **teaspoon dried oregano**
- ¼ **teaspoon paprika**
- ⅛ **teaspoon garlic powder**
- ⅛ **teaspoon ground mustard**

In a small bowl, whisk together all of the ingredients. Drizzle over sandwiches.

RASPBERRY LEMONADE CONCENTRATE

Here's a homemade concentrate that will allow you to enjoy a refreshing summer beverage any time of year. Raspberries balance the tartness from lemons.

—TASTE OF HOME TEST KITCHEN

PREP: 30 MIN. • **PROCESS:** 10 MIN.
MAKES: 5 PINTS (4 SERVINGS EACH)

- 4 **pounds fresh raspberries (about 14 cups)**
- 6 **cups sugar**
- 4 **cups lemon juice**
   Chilled tonic water or ginger ale
   Ice cubes

1. Place raspberries in a food processor; cover and process until blended. Strain raspberries, reserving juice. Discard seeds. Place juice in a Dutch oven; stir in the sugar and lemon juice. Heat over medium-high heat to 190°. Do not boil.

2. Remove from heat; skim off foam. Carefully ladle hot mixture into five hot 1-pint jars, leaving ¼-in. headspace. Wipe the rims; screw on bands until fingertip tight.

3. Place the jars into canner with simmering water, ensuring that they are completely covered with water. Bring to a boil; process for 10 minutes. Remove jars and cool.

TO USE CONCENTRATE *Mix 1 pint concentrate with 1 pint tonic water. Serve over ice.*

NOTE *The processing time listed is for altitudes of 1,000 feet or less. Add 1 minute to the processing time for each 1,000 feet of additional altitude.*

RASPBERRY HONEY VINEGAR

For an extra-special gift to give party guests, pair the ruby-red vinegar with a recipe that highlights its flavor.

—DEBBIE JONES HOLLYWOOD, MD

START TO FINISH: 25 MIN.
MAKES: 1¼ CUPS

- **2   cups fresh or frozen unsweetened raspberries**
- **¾ cup cider vinegar**
- **⅓ cup honey**
- **1   cinnamon stick**

In a saucepan, bring all ingredients to a boil. Reduce heat; cover and simmer 20 minutes. Remove from the heat; cool. Strain through a cheesecloth. Pour into a sterilized bottle or decanter. Cover and refrigerate until ready to use.

APRICOT LEATHER

PREP: 50 MIN. • **BAKE:** 2 HOURS
MAKES: 4 DOZEN PIECES

- **8   ounces dried apricots**
- **2   tablespoons sugar**
- **1   drop almond extract**
     Confectioners' sugar

1. Place apricots in a small saucepan and cover with water by 1 in. Bring to a boil. Reduce heat; simmer, uncovered, 30 minutes or until soft. Drain apricots and cool slightly.

2. Place apricots in a blender; add the sugar. Cover and process until smooth. Add extract.

3. Preheat oven to 175°. Line two shallow baking pans with silicone baking mats. Spoon half of apricot mixture onto each baking mat, spreading to form a 12x8-in. rectangle; repeat with remaining fruit. Bake 2 to 2½ hours or until almost dry to the touch. Cool completely on a wire rack.

4. Transfer to a cutting board; dust both sides with confectioners' sugar. Cut into ½x8-in. strips; roll up. Store in an airtight container in a cool dry place.

NOTE *If baked fruit sticks to the knife, air-dry 15-20 minutes, then slice and roll.*

FOOD TRIVIA!
Fruit leathers are believed to have originated in ancient Mesopotamia. Chewy fruit leathers are enjoyed by both kids and adults.

Since it isn't sticky, this tasty, nutritious snack is perfect to take along anywhere. Kids will want to share it with friends. —**PATSY FAYE STEENBOCK** RIVERTON, WY

❶ ROASTED RED PEPPER SPREAD

Here's a flavorful spread that will liven up any sandwich. Try tossing it with salad greens before adding to your sandwich.
—*TASTE OF HOME* TEST KITCHEN

START TO FINISH: 10 MIN.
MAKES: ¾ CUP

- 1 cup roasted sweet red pepper strips, drained
- 2 teaspoons olive oil
- 1 teaspoon balsamic vinegar
- ½ teaspoon sugar
- ½ teaspoon onion powder
- ⅛ teaspoon salt
- ⅛ teaspoon pepper

Place all ingredients in a small food processor; cover and process until pureed. Store in the refrigerator.
NOTE *This recipe was tested with Vlasic roasted red pepper strips.*

❷ LEMON-GARLIC SPREAD

The lemon-garlic combo complements most any meat or seafood sandwich.
—*TASTE OF HOME* TEST KITCHEN

START TO FINISH: 10 MIN.
MAKES: ½ CUP

- ⅓ cup mayonnaise
- 2 tablespoons olive oil
- 1 tablespoon red wine vinegar
- 1 garlic clove, minced
- 1 teaspoon grated lemon peel
- ¼ teaspoon lemon-pepper seasoning

In a small bowl, whisk all ingredients until blended. Store in the refrigerator.

❸ CREAMY HERB SPREAD

This herb condiment is ideal for chicken, turkey or veggie handhelds.

—TASTE OF HOME TEST KITCHEN

START TO FINISH: 5 MIN. • **MAKES:** ½ CUP

- 1 **package (3 ounces) cream cheese, softened**
- ¼ **cup loosely packed basil leaves**
- ¼ **cup mayonnaise**
- 1 **tablespoon minced fresh parsley**
- ½ **teaspoon cider vinegar**
- ⅛ **teaspoon pepper**
   Dash salt

Process all ingredients in a small food processor; until blended. Store in the refrigerator.

GRAPE LEATHER

Instead of giving your kids packaged fruit snacks, offer them fruit leather!

—TASTE OF HOME TEST KITCHEN

PREP: 25 MIN. • **BAKE:** 2½ HOURS + COOLING
MAKES: 6 SERVINGS

- 1½ **pounds seedless red grapes**
- 2 **tablespoons sugar**
- 1 **tablespoon lemon juice**

1. Sort and wash grapes; remove stems. Place grapes in a steamer basket; place in a large saucepan over 1 in. of water. Bring to a boil; cover and steam for 15 minutes or until soft.

2. Puree grapes in a blender or food processor. Strain grapes through a food mill into a small bowl; discard skin. Stir in sugar and lemon juice.

3. Line a 15x10x1-in. baking pan with parchment paper. Spread mixture evenly onto parchment paper. Bake at 200° 2½ to 3½ hours or until fruit leather feels slightly sticky. Cool completely.

4. Transfer fruit leather to a new 15x10-in. sheet of parchment paper. Roll up leather in parchment paper jelly-roll style, starting with a short side (do not unroll). Cut into six 1½-in. pieces. Store in an airtight container in a cool dry place up to 1 month.

HERBED VINEGAR

PREP: 10 MIN. + STANDING
MAKES: 2 CUPS

- ½ cup minced fresh basil
- ¼ cup minced fresh tarragon
- 2 cups white wine vinegar
  Fresh basil and/or tarragon sprigs, optional

1. Place basil and tarragon in a small glass bowl. Heat vinegar just until simmering; pour over herbs. Cool to room temperature. Cover and let stand in a cool dark place 5 days.
2. Strain and discard herbs. Pour vinegar into a decorative bottle or sterilized jar. If desired, add basil and/or tarragon sprigs. Store in a cool dark place for up to 6 months.

> Herb vinegar would be a great addition to your favorite salad dressing or it could be used in place of vinegar in any recipe. The terrific flavors of tarragon and basil really shine through.
> —*TASTE OF HOME* TEST KITCHEN

STRAWBERRY ORANGE VINEGAR

Add a splash of this pretty homemade vinegar to your next salad. Use your favorite salad greens or a ready-to-serve package to keep things simple.

—*TASTE OF HOME* TEST KITCHEN

PREP: 10 MIN.
COOK: 10 MIN. + STANDING
MAKES: 1⅔ CUPS

- 1 **medium orange**
- 2 **cups white wine vinegar**
- 2 **tablespoons sugar**
- 2 **cups sliced fresh strawberries**

1. Using a citrus zester, peel rind from orange in long narrow strips (being careful not to remove pith). In a large saucepan, heat vinegar and sugar to just below the boiling point. Place the strawberries in a warm sterilized quart jar; add heated vinegar mixture and orange peel. Cover and let stand in a cool dark place 10 days.

2. Strain the mixture through a cheesecloth; discard pulp and orange rind. Pour into a sterilized pint jar. Seal tightly. Store in the refrigerator up to 6 months.

FOOD TRIVIA!

A simple vinaigrette is an easy way to dress a salad. Whisk one part vinegar with two to three parts oil, then add a dash or two of salt and pepper.

CHOCOLATE-DIPPED APPLE RINGS

These apple treats are a staple in my Christmas goody packages. Sometimes I add an ⅛ teaspoon of cayenne to the cinnamon mixture for a little extra kick.
—**LAURIE BOCK** LYNDEN, WA

PREP: 30 MIN.
BAKE: 2 HOURS 20 MIN. + STANDING
MAKES: ABOUT 6 DOZEN

- 2 **pounds medium apples**
- 1½ **cups sugar**
- 2 **tablespoons ground cinnamon**
- 12 **ounces semisweet chocolate, chopped**
  Assorted sprinkles or small candies

1. Preheat oven to 225°. Core apples and cut crosswise into ⅛-in. slices. In a shallow bowl, mix sugar and cinnamon.

Dip apple slices in sugar mixture to coat both sides; shake off excess. Arrange in a single layer on parchment paper-lined baking sheets.

2. Bake 1½ hours. Turn; bake 50-60 minutes longer or until apples are dry and slightly shriveled. Remove from pans to wire racks to cool completely.

3. In top of a double boiler or a metal bowl over simmering water, melt the chocolate; stir until smooth. Dip the apple slices in chocolate; allow excess to drip off. Place on parchment or waxed paper; decorate with sprinkles as desired. Let stand until set. Store in airtight containers.

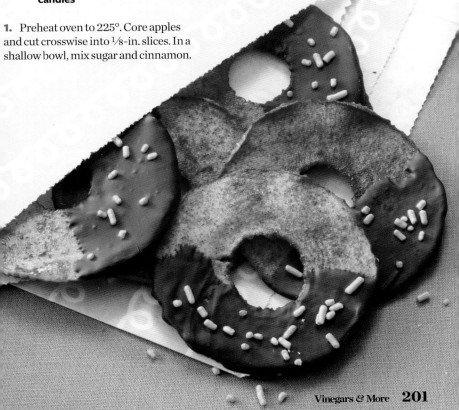

RASPBERRY VINEGAR

Looking for something tasty to make with fresh raspberries? This dressing adds summer-fresh flavor to salads.

—FRANCY NIGHTINGALE ISSAQUAH, WA

PREP: 20 MIN. + STANDING
MAKES: 4 CUPS

- **3 cups fresh raspberries**
- **4 cups white wine vinegar**
- **½ cup sugar**

1. Rinse the berries and air-dry on paper towels. Place berries in a 6-cup jar; set aside. In large saucepan, combine vinegar and sugar; bring almost to a boil over low heat, stirring constantly, until sugar is dissolved. Do not boil.

2. Pour hot vinegar mixture over berries; cover jar tightly and let stand at room temperature 48 hours. Strain through several layers of cheesecloth into a sterilized bottle or jar. Seal tightly with a cork or lid. Store in cool dark place.

TERIYAKI BEEF JERKY

Jerky is a portable, chewy snack. You can make your own with our recipe. The savory meat has a bit of heat from the red pepper flakes.

—TASTE OF HOME TEST KITCHEN

PREP: 40 MIN. + MARINATING • **BAKE:** 4 HOURS
MAKES: 8 SERVINGS

- 1 **beef flank steak (1½ to 2 pounds)**
- ⅔ **cup reduced-sodium soy sauce**
- ⅔ **cup Worcestershire sauce**
- ¼ **cup honey**
- 3 **teaspoons coarsely ground pepper**
- 2 **teaspoons onion powder**
- 2 **teaspoons garlic powder**
- 1½ **teaspoons crushed red pepper flakes**
- 1 **teaspoon liquid smoke**

1. Trim all visible fat from steak. Freeze, covered, 30 minutes or until firm. Slice steak along the grain into long ⅛-in.-thick strips.

2. Transfer to a large resealable plastic bag. In a small bowl, whisk remaining ingredients; add to beef. Seal bag and turn to coat. Refrigerate 2 hours or overnight, turning occasionally.

3. Preheat oven to 170°. Transfer beef and marinade to a large saucepan; bring to a boil. Reduce heat; simmer 5 minutes. Using tongs, remove beef from marinade; drain on paper towels. Discard marinade.

4. Arrange beef strips in single layer on wire racks placed on 15x10x1-in. baking pans. Dry in oven 4-5 hours or until beef becomes dry and leathery, rotating pans occasionally. (Or use a commercial dehydrator, following the manufacturer's directions.)

5. Remove from oven; cool completely. Using paper towels, blot any beads of oil on jerky. For best quality and longer storage, store jerky, covered, in refrigerator or freezer.

STICKY NOTES

General Index

Alpha Index

208